Seven pioneers of psychology

The past 100 years have yielded unique and powerful contributions to our understanding of human behaviour and the mind. William James, Fred Skinner, Jean Piaget, Sigmund Freud, Konrad Lorenz, Niko Tinbergen and Francis Galton all played key roles in the development of this understanding.

Freud's concepts have radically altered our view of ourselves, providing perhaps the most widely accepted idiom for discussing personality and interpersonal relationships. William James' 1890 classic, *Principles of Psychology*, laid out the agenda for theory and research that has dominated psychological science ever since. Sir Francis Galton was a polymath perhaps best known for his work on heredity and as the founder of eugenics. In psychology he undertook the first enquiry into intelligence, devised the word association test and investigated mental imagery. Piaget initiated the study of children's intellectual development, whilst Lorenz and Tinbergen were the founders of ethology – an approach to the study of behaviour that recognizes the equal relevance of evolutionary, functional, developmental and environmental influences on behaviour. Fred Skinner viewed behaviour as a natural phenomenon in its own right, not as an appendage to physiological or cognitive events. His analyses ranged widely, from experimental studies of learning in animals, theoretical analyses of verbal behaviour and human consciousness to a reappraisal of cultural and societal issues from a behavioural perspective.

In *Behaviour and Mind* six of today's leading scholars review the contributions made by these outstanding figures. They do so in a way that is both entertaining and enlightening and which is accessible to a wide audience.

Ray Fuller is Head of the Department of Psychology at Trinity College, Dublin.

Seven pioneers of psychology
Behaviour and mind

Edited by Ray Fuller

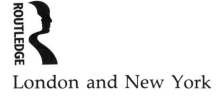

London and New York

First published 1995
by Routledge
11 New Fetter Lane, London EC4P 4EE

Simultaneously published in the USA and Canada
by Routledge
29 West 35th Street, New York, NY 10001

© 1995 Selection and editorial matter, Ray Fuller;
individual chapters, the contributors

Typeset in Palatino by Mews Photosetting,
Beckenham, Kent
Printed and bound in Great Britain by
Biddles Ltd, Guildford and King's Lynn

British Library Cataloguing in Publication Data
A catalogue record for this book is available from
the British Library

Library of Congress Cataloging in Publication Data
A catalog record for this book has been requested

ISBN 0-415-09979-X (hbk)
ISBN 0-415-09980-3 (pbk)

Contents

Figures

Contributors

Professor Derek E. Blackman is a past president of the British Psychological Society and former dean of the Faculty of Economic and Social Studies, University College, Cardiff. He was a member of the DHS Working Party on Ethical Guidelines for Programmes of Behaviour Modification in Hospitals and of the Home Office Advisory Committee on Animal Experiments. He served as the advisor for psychology for the Universities' Funding Council, and was editor of the *British Journal of Psychology* 1983–9. He is currently chief examiner for the International Baccalaureate Organization. He has authored or edited seven books covering contemporary behaviourism, psychopharmacology, psychology and law, and animal welfare and law. He currently holds a chair in the school of psychology, University of Wales College of Cardiff.

Professor Peter E. Bryant took his BA at Cambridge University and his PhD at the University of London, Institute of Psychiatry. In 1964 he worked in Piaget's department at the Institut des Sciences de l'Education, University of Geneva, and in 1967 took up an appointment as university lecturer in the Department of Experimental Psychology, Oxford University. Since 1980 he has been Watts Professor of Psychology there. His books (as author, co-author or editor) include *Perception and Understanding in Young Children; Piaget: Issues and Experiments; Rhyme and Reason in Reading and Spelling; Children's Reading Problems;*

Phonological Skills and Learning to Read; and *Causes of Development*. He is a fellow of St John's College, Oxford, of Wolfson College, Oxford, and of the Royal Society.

Professor Derek W. Forrest held the chair of psychology at Trinity College, Dublin, from 1967 until his retirement in 1993. Before coming to Ireland in 1962 in order to found the Trinity Psychology Department he had worked in applied experimental research at Farnborough and had lectured at Bedford College, London University. Author of some forty papers in psychology journals, his major work is his biography, *Francis Galton: The Life and Work of a Victorian Genius*. He has recently completed a history of hypnotism and has begun work on a biography of Charcot. He is now a fellow emeritus of Trinity College, Dublin.

Professor Robert A. Hinde served as a pilot in Coastal Command (UK) from 1941 to 1945 and then read zoology at St John's College, Cambridge. He took a DPhil at Balliol College, Oxford, where he was much influenced by Niko Tinbergen. He then assisted W.H. Thorpe to establish the Department of Animal Behaviour at Madingley, Cambridge. He was subsequently appointed a Royal Society research professor and honorary director of an MRC Unit at Madingley. He has been a fellow, steward and tutor at St John's College, of which he is currently master. He is Commander of the Order of the British Empire, a fellow of the Royal Society, a foreign honorary member of the American Academy of Arts and Sciences, and a foreign associate of the UN National Academy of Sciences. He is an honorary fellow of Trinity College, Dublin, and Balliol College, Oxford, and holds honorary doctorates from the Université Libre, Brussels; Paris (Nanterre); Stirling; and Goteborg.

Professor Jerome L. Singer received his doctorate in clinical psychology from the University of Pennsylvania. He is a fellow of the APA, the American Association for the Advancement of Science and the New York Academy of Sciences. He is a former president of the Eastern Psychological Association, of the Division of Personality and Social Psychology of the APA, and of the American Association for the Study of Mental Imagery, and chair of the Board of Scientific Affairs of the APA. He has written or edited more than fifteen books, including *The Inner World of Daydreaming: The Stream of Consciousness; Television, Imagination and Aggression; The House of Make-believe: Children's Play and the Developing Imagination; The Human Personality; Repression and Dissociation.* Currently he is editor of *Imagination, Cognition and Personality* and senior consultant to the Open Laboratory of Conscious and Unconscious Mental Processes at the University of California Langley Porter Psychiatric Institute. He is professor of psychology of Yale University and co-director (with Dorothy G. Singer) of the Yale University Family Television Research and Consultation Center.

Dr Anthony Storr was educated at Winchester, at Christ's College, Cambridge, and at Westminster Hospital. He qualified as a doctor in 1944 and subsequently specialized in psychiatry. From 1974 until his retirement in 1984, he was consultant psychotherapist at the Warneford Hospital, Oxford, where he was chiefly engaged in teaching. His books include *The Integrity of the Personality; Human Destructiveness; Jung; The Dynamics of Creation; The Art of Psychotherapy; Solitude; Freud; Churchill's Black Dog;* and *Music and the Mind.* He is an emeritus fellow of Green College, Oxford, and a fellow of the Royal College of Physicians, of the Royal College of Psychiatrists and of the Royal Society of Literature.

Preface

In 1992, Trinity College, Dublin, celebrated the four hundredth anniversary of its founding by the Royal Charter of Queen Elizabeth I. The occasion was marked over several months by a procession of academic and social events, involving many guests from home and abroad, thousands of visiting academics and alumni, the entire staff of the college from porter to provost, and at times a good cross-section of the citizens of Dublin. The contribution of the Department of Psychology to these proceedings, while not altogether ignoring the social, focused on a number of academic events. This book is the result of one such.

It is no easy task for psychologists to know best how to salute an ancient institution when their separate discipline can claim barely a quarter of the lifespan of that institution and their academic department significantly less: it was but thirty years in existence in 1992. The 'apprentice' can hardly tell the 'master' what a good job he has done. And so it was with a ready acceptance that my colleagues took to the suggestion that we invite a group of scholars each to present in a public lecture a review of the contribution of a great scientist to our understanding of behaviour and mental processes. But which great scientists? To simplify the task we omitted from consideration those still living, and from a list of nineteen selected: James, Freud, Piaget, Skinner and Lorenz. Identifying accomplished scholars to review the significance of the work of these scientists was a much easier task and led to the authors you will read between these covers: Singer, Storr, Bryant, Blackman and Hinde.

But the process did not stop at that. Derek Forrest, who retired as the first and only holder of the chair of psychology in Trinity College in 1993, was invited to write an introduction to this book. He suggested that a chapter on Galton might be appropriate, as Galton had anticipated in his work a range of concepts (such as unconscious mental processes and mental imagery) which others later took up and developed. And so Galton was included not only in the book, but also as a welcome extension of the original lecture series. And finally Robert Hinde suggested that a review of Lorenz which included Tinbergen might be more complete, as the ideas, methods and lives of these two men were so closely intertwined. Thus was the public lecture series established and by any standard it was a success, with over one thousand attending.

The achievements of Galton covered a wide spectrum of the sciences. An explorer and geographer, meteorologist, statistician, anthropologist and psychologist, he is perhaps best known as the founder of eugenics and as a contributor to our knowledge of human heredity. Derek Forrest's 'Galton' is a gentleman of independent means who was free to pursue his creative scientific genius, giving us the weather map, fingerprinting as a method of identifying criminals, and a host of psychological concepts and methods. These included the first enquiry into intelligence, the investigation of mental imagery and the invention of the word association test.

James' classic *Principles of Psychology*, published in 1890, laid out the agenda for theory and research that has dominated psychological science ever since. He addressed with insight, sensitivity and precision such fundamental issues as attention, memory, emotion and the stream of consciousness. Jerome Singer's 'James' relates the study of the stream of human consciousness both to the creative work of another James, James Joyce, and also to his own life-long work using the methods of scientific enquiry to enrich our understanding of this fundamental aspect of mental life.

None could deny that Freud's original and persuasive concepts have radically altered our view of ourselves, providing perhaps the most widely accepted idiom for discussing personality and interpersonal relationships and having major effects on both art and literature. Anthony Storr's 'Freud' reveals the dynamic relationship between Freud's obsessive personality characteristics and his theoretical concepts. He also describes how Freud shares with the ethologists the centrality of the concept of instinct in driving behaviour; a position made more tenable because of the 'paradigm shift' introduced by Darwin's concept of the human as part of the animal kingdom and not 'uniquely created in God's image'.

Lorenz and Tinbergen were the founders of ethology, an approach to the study of behaviour that recognizes the equal relevance of evolutionary, functional, developmental and environmental influences in behaviour. Robert Hinde's 'Lorenz' and 'Tinbergen' provide a review of the early concepts of these pioneering ethologists and reveal how they stimulated enquiry into major issues of behaviour which go far beyond the boundaries of their own discipline. The concepts of ethology have spread to psychology, psychiatry, anthropology, neurophysiology and other disciplines.

Skinner's theoretical stance was based on the view that behaviour should be considered as a natural phenomenon in its own right, not as an appendage to physiological or cognitive events. His contribution ranged over experimental studies of learning in animals, the theoretical analysis of verbal behaviour and human consciousness, and the use of behavioural methods in applied psychology, and included a reappraisal of cultural and societal issues from a behavioural perspective. Derek Blackman's 'Skinner' clarifies a host of misconceptions regarding Skinner's theoretical position which have persisted to the present day, and paints a portrait of a civilized gentleman who lived out his own theory.

Piaget can be credited with initiating the study of children's intellectual development and his ideas still dominate virtually all current research on this topic. His theory – that logical skills develop during childhood – is still controversial, but his empirical research amply demonstrated how radically children's solutions to logical and mathematical problems change as they grow older. Peter Bryant's 'Piaget' provides a lucid and critical review of Piaget's developmental concepts and concludes with an accessible evaluation of his methods of enquiry.

Something of the pleasure of hearing these authors speak in Trinity's quatercentenary year will, I hope, be shared by the reader.

Ray Fuller
Dublin

Plate 1 Francis Galton (1822–1911)
By permission of Department of Psychology, University College
London

1 Francis Galton (1822–1911)

Derek W. Forrest

Francis Galton (1822–1911), cousin of Charles Darwin, was born at Sparkbrook, Birmingham, and trained as a doctor at Birmingham General Hospital and King's College, London, interrupting his medical career to take a mathematics degree at Trinity College, Cambridge. He forsook medicine to travel in Egypt and Syria and to explore south-west Africa. On his return he was awarded the gold medal of the Royal Geographical Society and published Tropical South Africa *(1853). In the same year he married Louisa Butler, a member of the distinguished academic family. Turning his attention to meteorology he established the theory of anticyclones (*Meteorographica, 1863) *and produced the first weather maps. His interest in heredity dates from the 1860s and extended throughout his life; it resulted in his major work,* Hereditary Genius *(1869), and in* English Men of Science: Their Nature and Nurture *(1874), his last substantial contribution being* Natural Inheritance *(1889). By this date his work in statistics had led him to the concept of correlation and its application to human variation. This discovery emerged from a large-scale programme of physical and psychological measurement carried out by his anthropometric laboratory, established in 1884. One practical consequence of the work of the laboratory was the finding that fingerprints were an ideal index of personal identity (*Finger Prints, 1892*), and he persuaded Scotland Yard to adopt them. Galton's psychological work extended over a period of approximately fifteen years, much of it incorporated in his* Inquiries into Human Faculty and Its Development *(1883). This book includes his important papers on word association and imagery, but also ranges widely over such varied topics as sensory acuity, composite portraiture, the efficacy of prayer, free will, gregariousness, and the domestication of animals. Through this work he established his reputation as the founder of*

*individual psychology and as the originator of the mental testing
movement. Galton was a prolific researcher, inventor and polymath
with an output of over 340 papers and books. He served on many
committees and received many awards, including the Copley Medal
of the Royal Society and a knighthood. The latter part of his
life was mainly devoted to the advocacy of eugenics, his own
term for the selective breeding of good stock, and it was for the
promulgation of related research that he bequeathed most of his
fortune.*

Francis Galton was born in 1822 and died in 1911. He lived
therefore during the period when it could be argued that
individualism and liberalism were more prominent in
Britain than elsewhere. Within such a *Zeitgeist* it is not
surprising that he should have initiated the study of
differences among individuals, on account of which he has
long held an honoured place in the history of psychology.

However, it is misleading to consider Galton as primarily
a psychologist. Less than one quarter of his published output can be regarded as having psychological relevance.
Some appreciation of his other interests is important, not
only in understanding the man himself but also in placing
his psychological work in a broader perspective.

The youngest son of Samuel Galton, a successful Quaker
banker, and Violetta Darwin, Charles Darwin's aunt,
Francis achieved some notoriety for his precociousness as
a child, rivalling John Stuart Mill in this regard. He was
pushed by his father into a medical training at the age of
16, interrupted by three years at Cambridge where he read
mathematics. He had to be content with a pass degree on
account of his first breakdown with an obsessional illness.
He likened it on this occasion to a mill working inside his
head; small and apparently intractable problems obsessed
him day and night, and he was forced to drop all intellectual work. However, after a break, he was able to return
to his medical studies and kept at them until the death of
his father released him from what had become an obliga-
tion. He was now free to live on his inheritance and was
never to undertake paid employment.

Obsessional difficulties of a milder kind dogged Galton throughout his life and were influential in structuring the nature of his future research. He was always to be unhappy with data that could not easily be quantified and sought for new techniques of measurement to bring material under control. 'Whenever you can, count' became his favourite dictum. His obsessionality also showed in the tight rein he kept on his emotional life and the intellectualizing defence he frequently adopted.

Galton first attracted the notice of Victorian scientific circles with an account of an exploration of south-west Africa which he had undertaken between 1850 and 1852. His careful use of surveying and astronomical instruments led to exact mapping of unknown terrain, a feat for which the Royal Geographical Society awarded him their gold medal. This distinction was shortly followed by election to the council of that body, election to the Athenaeum club, and fellowship of the Royal Society. Thus began Galton's involvement in the London scientific scene; having few domestic interests and enjoying the company of other men, he made many valuable acquaintances who were to help in furthering his later research.

An account of his African travels appeared in book form soon after his return. It contained a lively account of his expedition, omitting the technical details. One unusual use of his surveying instruments was, however, recorded. He was staying with some missionaries when he encountered a Hottentot beauty:

I profess to be a scientific man, and was exceedingly anxious to obtain accurate measurements of her shape; but there was a difficulty in doing this. I did not know a word of Hottentot, and could never therefore explain to the lady what the object of my footrule could be; and I really dared not ask my worthy missionary host to interpret for me. The object of my admiration stood under a tree, and was turning herself about to all points of the compass, as ladies who wish to be admired usually do. Of a sudden my eye fell upon my sextant;

the bright thought struck me, and I took a series of observations upon her figure in every direction, up and down, crossways, diagonally, and so forth, and I registered them carefully upon an outline drawing for fear of any mistake. This being done, I boldly pulled out my measuring tape, and measured the distance from where I was to the place where she stood, and having thus obtained both base and angles, I worked out the results by trigonometry and logarithms.

(Galton 1853: 54)

Galton later compiled a further book based on his own travels and those of many others. Under the title *The Art of Travel* it was to go to eight editions, a reprint of the fifth appearing as recently as 1971. This little book shows Galton at his ingenious best. Packed with practical information on navigation, hunting, fishing, shelter, bedding, the management of animals, and so on, it provides a prospective traveller with useful, if sometimes bizarre, information for a successful journey. A few examples follow:

Fording a stream:
In fording a swift stream, carry heavy stones in your hand, for you require weight to resist the force of the current.... Streams cannot be forded if their depth exceeds 3 feet for men or 4 feet for horses.

(Galton 1872: 107–8)

Swimming with a horse:
Lead him along a steep bank, and push him sideways, suddenly into the water: having fairly started him, jump in yourself, seize his tail, and let him tow you across. If he turns his head with the intention of changing his course, splash water in his face with your right or left hand, as the case may be, holding the tail with one hand and splashing with the other; and you will, in this way, direct him just as you like.

(Galton 1872: 85)

Blistered feet:
To prevent the feet from blistering, it is a good plan to soap the inside of the stocking before setting out, making a thick lather all over it. A raw egg broken into a boot, before putting it on, greatly softens the leather.
(Galton 1872: 19)

Emetics:
For want of proper physic, drink a charge of gunpowder in a tumblerful of warm water or soap suds, and tickle the throat.
(Galton 1872: 15)

Keeping dogs at bay:
A watchdog usually desists from flying at a stranger when he seats himself quietly on the ground, like Ulysses.
(Galton 1872: 254)

And if you want to keep your clothes dry in a tropical downpour, Galton provides the simple solution that you should take them off and sit on them (Galton 1872: 119).

Galton's interest in the mathematics and techniques of measurement led him to concentrate within the field of geography on mapping and meteorological observation, and it was here that he made his first notable contribution to science. He had collated barometric readings from weather stations in Europe and mapped them. He was perhaps fortunate to happen upon a sequence of events in which clockwise winds were flowing from a high-pressure area – a reversal of the then-known cyclonic condition – to which he gave the name 'anticyclone'. It was some years before technical printing difficulties were to be overcome and Galton's innovation, the weather map, with which we are now so familiar, could first appear in *The Times* in 1875.

The involvement in geographical and meteorological matters continued throughout his life; he was still active in the affairs of the Royal Geographical Society and the Meteorological Council in his seventies, although his participation became increasingly of an administrative nature. During his forties, his research interests began to focus on heredity, a change which he ascribed to Darwin's influence. *The Origin of Species* had appeared in 1859 and had strongly affected Galton. The book, he said, 'made a marked epoch in my mental development'. He was 'encouraged by the new views to pursue many enquiries that had long interested' him and 'which clustered around the central topics of heredity' (Galton 1908: 288).

I have speculated elsewhere that a more personal motivation may also have been influential (Forrest 1974). Soon after his return from Africa, Galton had married Louisa Butler, a woman of his own age (31) and a member of a distinguished academic family. The beginnings of Galton's research into heredity began when it must have become evident that his own marriage was to prove infertile. He claimed that it was at Cambridge that he had first noticed that academic talent appeared to run in the families of his contemporaries. The Butler–Galton connection promised so much but seemed certain to lead to nothing. His speculations over the fruit of his marital union were perhaps diverted into a broader context, and he began to collect data for his first important book, *Hereditary Genius* (Galton 1869). This book also marks the beginning of his psychological work, which was rarely separable from an overriding hereditarian concern.

The thesis of the book is, of course, that genius, or 'talent', to use the word Galton later preferred, is genetically rather than environmentally determined. Galton's first problem lay in the selection of talented people for investigation. He solved that by choosing a public reputation as an indication that the person must be highly talented. People with a public reputation are given obituaries, and by counting the number of obituaries in *The Times* and comparing it with the number of middle-aged persons alive in the British Isles at the time, Galton was able to estimate that 1 in 4,000 obtained such a reputation. It was people of this rarity with whom he was concerned in his book. In a typically Galtonian simile he tells us that never more than 4,000 stars are visible on the clearest of nights and his subjects are as rare as the brightest one of these stars.

By an examination of lists of famous people in the fields of law, politics, science, art, sport and so on, Galton was able to trace their relatives in order to ascertain how many of them were bright enough stars to merit obituaries. He could then calculate the percentage of talented people in various degrees of kinship to the initial famous person. Figure 1.1 shows the results in the case of judges, and similar findings were obtained with other professions. There seemed to be a regular increase in ability up to its culmination in the most eminent member and a regular decrease in those who followed: 'In the first case the marriages have been consentient to its production, in the latter they have been incapable of preserving it' (Galton 1869: 123).

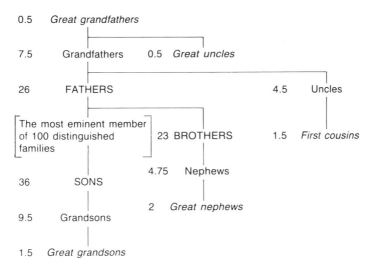

Figure 1.1 Percentage of eminent men in each degree of kinship to the most gifted member of distinguished families
Source: Galton 1869: 123

The regularity in his statistics made him feel sure that he was on the verge of discovering a law, and indeed later he was to describe such a law in which the two parents contributed one half of an individual's total heredity, the four grandparents one quarter, and so on with more remote ancestors (Galton 1898). While this seems quaint today, it must be remembered that the rediscovery of Mendel's work was not to occur until 1900, and discovery of the heredity mechanism was to escape all Galton's research efforts, which were to include the breeding of sweet peas and moths in addition to the compilation of human statistics.

Of course, the kinsmen of the eminent persons who made up the subject matter of *Hereditary Genius* often achieved fame in other walks of life than that of their distinguished relative. Galton believed that he could point to three inherited characteristics necessary for success in life, namely, intelligence, zeal and a capacity for hard work. To the extent that they inherited a combination of these, the relatives of the eminent would achieve a public reputation of their own.

Galton fully realized that he had been unable to assess the relative contribution of the environment to the success of his subjects. The idea that he might be able to use twins to make the relevant separation of environment from heredity occurred to him some five years later. Through the use of a questionnaire he was able to establish to his own satisfaction that identical twins as distinct from fraternal twins retained great similarities in their abilities, tastes and dispositions throughout their lives despite their different life histories. He writes:

> There is no escape from the conclusion that nature prevails enormously over nurture when the differences of nurture do not exceed what is commonly found among persons of the same rank of society and in the same country.
>
> (Galton 1876: 404)

The final qualification is very important. It is one that many critics of Galton's conclusions have failed to note. It must be said it is also one that Galton himself seems sometimes to have forgotten.

In the second part of *Hereditary Genius* Galton writes about the enormous differences in every ability that one cannot help observing among individuals. And he claims that it should be possible to arrange people in order along a continuum of a particular ability and to calculate the number of people at each point. This argument involves an extrapolation from the findings of the Belgian astronomer, Quetelet, who had found not only that errors made by astronomers taking observations approximated to a Gaussian or 'normal' curve, but that various physical measurements, such as height and chest circumference, were similarly distributed. Galton argued that it should follow that head size, brain weight and the number of nerve fibres will be normally distributed. Is it then such a jump to presume that the functions dependent on these tissues will also be normally distributed?

The hypothesis was plausible but the difficulties in applying it enormous. Galton could find no way directly to measure ability – at least not the high levels of ability with which he was concerned – and, as we have seen, he had to be content with public reputation as a criterion of its possession; but that led only to a classification rather than to any type of scale. He tried to describe the probable characteristics of those further down the scale, such as the abilities of a foreman of an ordinary jury, and he was certain that those at the bottom end of the human scale would be far inferior to the top class of dogs!

He was later to speculate on a possible association between sensitivity and intellectual ability. He had no direct evidence for such an association, basing his opinion on reports of insensitivity to pain in two idiot boys, although he did think it obvious that 'the more perceptive our senses are of difference, the larger the field upon which our judgment and intelligence can act' (Galton 1883: 27). We are often told that Galton intended to design a test of intelligence using sensory measures, but I do not believe this idea ever occurred to him. As we shall see, it was certainly not the *raison-d'être* of his anthropometric laboratory.

Galton's difficulty in scaling the highest levels of intelligence is with us today. Any unidimensional scheme seems to founder in the face of the specialized talents of the intellectually gifted. In contrast, Alfred Binet's success may have had much to do with the nature of his task, which was to devise what has been described as a test of 'unintelligence' in order to enable the Parisian educational authorities to discriminate, from among the children receiving compulsory education, those who were unable to profit from it and who accordingly needed to go to special schools. Thus he was working at the lower end of the continuum where simple tasks were effective in making the relevant discrimination.

Galton's insight that the normal curve could be applied to mental abilities has been extraordinarily influential. The whole process of intelligence test construction involves the dropping or modification of items to ensure the normal distribution of test scores, because it is only then that the interpretation of a particular IQ can be made as a measure of comparative deviation from the population mean.

From the beginning, the implications of Galton's research were clear to him. An enormous effect might be produced upon the average ability of a nation if a policy of early marriage could be encouraged among the able. He gives, as an example, the fact that if talented couples were to marry eleven years earlier than those without talent, in a mere two centuries the mature descendants of the former would outnumber those of the latter in the ratio of 26 : 1. To encourage such early marriages he proposed that a government might provide grants for talented couples whilst denying support for the less talented. Another proposal, equally unlikely ever to be implemented, involved the award of extra marks in competitive examinations to those who came from meritorious families in order to give them a head start in their professional careers. Such proposals are a reflection of Galton's political naivety and lack of empathy with the ordinary citizen, deficiencies which were to vitiate many of his subsequent suggestions for hereditary improvement, or *eugenics* as he came to call it.

The eugenic concept became of paramount importance in Galton's thinking. It became an article of faith and filled the gap left by his loss of a Christian belief. He thought it might serve a similar purpose for other people as their belief in a God declined:

> It has, indeed, strong claims to become an orthodox religious tenet of the future, for Eugenics co-operates with the workings of Nature – What Nature does blindly, slowly and ruthlessly, man may do providently, quickly and kindly.
>
> (Galton 1909: 42)

If eugenic proposals were to be put into effect, it was necessary first to know the present mental and physical condition of the population, and only then might it prove possible to reach a consensus about the changes thought to be desirable. However, Galton thought there would be little doubt about such desiderata as good health, energy and ability. Strangely enough, he included two further qualities, manliness and courteous disposition, although whether both sexes were expected to exhibit these was not made clear (Galton 1909).

After a few false starts Galton adopted the laboratory approach to collect the necessary data. He equipped at his own expense an anthropometric laboratory, which was opened in conjunction with the International Health Exhibition held in South Kensington, London, in 1884–5. The laboratory was intended, as its name suggests, to be a source of human measurements. These were of a structural and dynamic type, and included standing and sitting height, weight, arm span, breathing capacity, strength of pull and squeeze, speed of punch, reaction time, acuity of vision and hearing, colour discrimination and judgements of length (Galton 1884). It is the psychologist's delusion of grandeur to believe that all these measurements were taken with some psychological end in view. The truth is that Galton simply wanted to establish a human balance sheet and to obtain some idea of the extent of variation in structure and function. The anthropologists certainly considered the work as falling within their province and invited Galton to be their president, an office he held from 1885 to 1889.

The laboratory was so successful in terms of the number of people who passed through it (nearly 10,000 in its year of opening) that it was decided to put it on a more permanent footing. Sited in the South Kensington Museum, it had a further life of eight years, during which time the opportunity was taken to record further measurements, which included hand size and fingerprints. The laboratory had two important outcomes, neither of direct psychological significance. In examining his data Galton was struck by the fact that the association between any two anthropometric variables posed the same problem with which he had been confronted in attempting to measure the resemblance between parents and offspring. In that work he had been led to the regression coefficient, and when he realized, in a sudden flash of inspiration, that his anthropometric variables had each to be expressed in terms of its own variability, he had reached the coefficient of correlation, his most significant statistical contribution (Galton 1888).

The other spin-off from the laboratory was in the field of personal identification. Having ascertained that positive correlations existed among several of his anthropometric measures, it became clear that the system of criminal identification devised by Alphonse Bertillon was not the optimal one. The system was based on a variety of bodily measurements, some of which, it now became clear, were not independent of one another. Galton cast about for other identifying marks that might be unique to the individual and finally hit upon fingerprints. The collection of fingerprints from his laboratory subjects enabled him to devise a method for their classification and to convince the relevant authorities that they should be used in criminal identification (Galton 1892). They were introduced by Scotland Yard on a trial basis and in conjunction with Bertillon's system in 1894, and finally adopted as the sole method of identification in 1901 after E.R. Henry had improved on Galton's classification.

The anthropometric laboratory did serve another function: it stimulated other researchers. Similar laboratories were opened in Oxford, Cambridge, Eton and Trinity College, Dublin. The Trinity laboratory was a mobile one which toured the west of Ireland during the long vacations, collecting data from relatively isolated ethnic groups (Forrest 1986). The anthropologist A.C. Haddon was the prime mover behind the Irish laboratory; he was later to be the leader of the famous Torres Straits Expedition which included William McDougall, C.S. Myers and W.H.R. Rivers among its members. Another individual who was impressed by Galton's approach to human measurement was James McKeen Cattell, whose first 'mental tests' were largely derived from Galton (Cattell 1890). It was thus Galton's example that lay behind the exact testing of simple functions which became so characteristic of the Columbia University tradition.

During the period between the publication of *Hereditary Genius* in 1867 and the opening of the anthropometric laboratory in 1884 Galton carried out psychological work of great originality and ingenuity. Most of this work was brought together in his *Inquiries into Human Faculty and Its Development* (Galton 1883), a book to which all students of psychology should be referred, as there is something there of interest to everyone; a book, I might add, which is badly in need of a modern reprint.

Galton's famous walk down Pall Mall, which he probably took in 1876, will be familiar to many psychologists. It was on that occasion that he tried to call up mental associations to the objects and scenes before his eyes. His initial admiration for the extensive net of associations he seemed to have at his command was substantially tempered, after repeating the walk, by the realization that the net was relatively rigid, with the same stimulus often producing the same response. An experimental approach suggested itself to him to ascertain if the vague mental phenomena could be caught by the 'firm grip of genuine statistical enquiry' (Galton 1879: 150). Thus was the word association test first conceived.

His choice of stimulus words was not optimal: they were the first 100 words taken from *Roget's Thesaurus* and included obscure and abstract terms. He exposed each word drawn at random from being hidden beneath a book and allowed himself four seconds in which to produce one or more responses. The whole experiment was repeated on three later occasions about a month apart (Forrest 1977). Galton attempted to classify both his stimulus words and responses, but little came of this. He was able to show that he more often gave verbal responses to abstract stimulus words, whereas other words produced either visual or motor imagery. An analysis in terms of the period of his life in which an association had first been formed proved to be much more fruitful. In about a quarter of his cases he was able to ascertain this fact, and was able to show that associations formed in his early years were likely to be those repeated on the later trials with the same list, whereas recent associations were less fixed and would vary from trial to trial. From this he inferred the 'large effect of early education in fixing our associations' (Galton 1879: 158).

Galton never published a full account of his 'psychometric experiments', as he called them. He had negotiated with Kegan Paul to publish a book on the topic but refused two years later on the grounds that his results were too bulky. It would be interesting to know what he must have discarded. Galton also never divulged the list of stimulus words nor his associations to them:

> It would be too absurd to print one's own singly. They lay bare the foundations of a man's thoughts with curious distinctness, and exhibit his mental anatomy with more vividness and truth than he would probably care to publish to the world.
>
> (Galton 1879: 62)

This paper concludes with the following prescient comment:

Perhaps the strangest impression left by these experiments regards the multifariousness of the work done by the mind in a state of half-unconsciousness, and the valid reason they afford for believing in the existence of still deeper strata of mental operations, sunk wholly below the level of consciousness, which may account for such mental phenomena as cannot otherwise be explained.

The fact that this paper was published in the journal *Brain* and that Sigmund Freud subscribed to that journal and quoted work by Hughlings Jackson from other issues of the same year leaves open the possibility that he read Galton's paper. At that date (1879) Freud was still doing histological work with Brücke and was not to hear Breuer's account of the case of Anna O. for another three years (Gay 1988). He never referred to Galton's discovery. It remains conjectural whether it played any part in the slow development of psychoanalytic free association from the earlier trials with hypnosis and suggestion.

In any case, other workers had pursued Galton's lead: Wundt's laboratory carried out controlled association experiments in 1882 and Cattell followed in 1889 with a paper on free association. The debt to Galton is clear even in Cattell's language when he writes that associations 'lay bare the mental life in a way that is startling and not always gratifying' (Cattell 1950: 537). Jung's subsequent use of the word association test as a clinical tool dates from 1906, but by then, of course, Freud had been using free association for more than a decade.

Galton immediately followed up his psychometric experiments with an enquiry into mental imagery. This work arose from a chance circumstance when, in discussion of his word association results with scientific friends, he discovered that some of them did not understand what he meant by a visual image. Individual differences in imagery seemed likely to prove a fruitful topic, and he devised a questionnaire.

Galton's 'breakfast table' is probably even better known than his 'walk'. The first questions posed to his respondents asked them to visualize a definite object such as their breakfast table of that morning and to estimate its degree of brightness, definition, completeness, colouring and extent. The range of responses was remarkable, from a complete absence of imagery to images of an hallucinatory quality. His statistical treatment of the results was not very enlightening, although he did seem to be justified in concluding that his group of scientific respondents were weak in imagery, a fact he ascribed to their habitual use of abstract thought (Galton 1880).

Galton himself was not a vivid visualizer and it was a remarkable example of sensitive enquiry that he was able to uncover the existence of 'number forms'. He used this term to describe the various patterns in which numbers were visualized by a small minority of the imaginally gifted (Figure 1.2). His writings on this matter, and on the personalization and colouring of digits, on synaesthesia and on the ocurrence of visions in sane persons, are still of topical interest (Galton 1883). Galton's other introspective work included a variety of self-observations, such as:

1 the effects of interfering with the autonomic control of his own breathing;
2 an attempt to induce paranoia in himself by investing everything he met with 'the imaginary attributes of a spy';
3 an attempt to understand idolatry by inducing religious awe to a picture of Punch;
4 six weeks of continuous self-observation to see if he had free will.

The other side to Francis Galton was the prolific inventor and acute observer and recorder of behaviour. Among his inventions of new locks and lamps, a printing telegraph, a rotary engine, a wave engine, a sun-signalling heliostat, diving spectacles and anthropometric equipment there were several items of psychological relevance. Best known was the *Galton Whistle*, which became a standard piece of equipment in early psychological laboratories. The whistle was

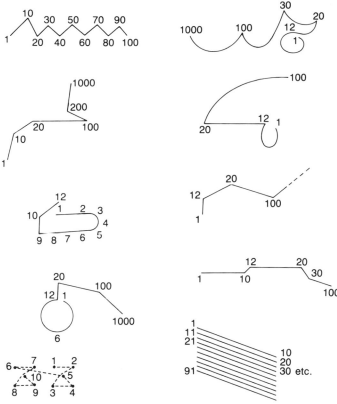

Figure 1.2 A variety of number forms
Source: Forrest 1974: 153

calibrated to enable the upper frequency of the auditory threshold to be measured. Galton secreted it in a walking stick and operated it by a rubber bulb in the handle so that it would remain inconspicuous when he visited the zoo to test the hearing of various animals. *Pocket registrators* were counting devices of various degrees of complexity which could be concealed in the pocket and operated by the fingers. Surreptitious statistics could be obtained by this means, such as estimates of the boredom of an audience by the frequency of their fidgets, or even the relative incidence of pretty girls in different towns in order to construct a beauty map of Britain. *Rapid-view instruments* were types of tachistoscope which Galton used to 'freeze' the movement of animals to enable the viewer to draw them afterwards. *Composite photography* was invented by Galton in order to obtain average representatives of different groups of people; for example, different races, families, sufferers from particular illnesses, criminals, vegetarians. He also used it to obtain the truest representation of single individuals through composites of several portraits of them.

The ideas poured out of him, some crack-brained, some still worth pursuing. If only all this creative energy could have been harnessed to one discipline, what might he have achieved? But Galton's personality make-up precluded such concentration; his obsessiveness led to bouts of data collection followed by carelessness in their treatment and boredom with that field of endeavour. Unable to commit himself to one science, he touched on many, and what he touched he illuminated. He once said, 'Great men have long boyhoods' (Galton 1865: 326). It was certainly true of him in his naivety, dash and momentary enthusiasms. As psychologists we have cause to be grateful for the few years he devoted to psychological matters and which merit his inclusion in this review of major historical contributors to our understanding of behaviour and mind.

REFERENCES

Cattell, J. McK. (1890) 'Mental tests and measurements', *Mind* 15: 373–81.
—— (1950) quoted by E.G. Boring, *A History of Experimental Psychology*, New York: Appleton-Century-Crofts.
Forrest, D.W. (1974) *Francis Galton: The Life and Work of a Victorian Genius*, London: Elek.
—— (1977) 'The first experiments on word association', *Bulletin of the British Psychological Society* 30: 40–2.
—— (1986) 'The anthropometric laboratory of Ireland', *American Psychologist* 41: 1384–5.
Galton, F. (1853) *Tropical South Africa*, London: Murray.
—— (1865) 'Hereditary talent and character', *Macmillan's Magazine* 12: 326.
—— (1869) *Hereditary Genius*, London: Macmillan.

—— (1872) *The Art of Travel*, 5th edition, London: Murray.

—— (1876) 'The history of twins, as a criterion of the relative powers of nature and nurture', *Journal of the Anthropological Institute* 5: 391–406.

—— (1879) 'Psychometric experiments', *Brain* 2: 149–62.

—— (1880) 'Statistics of mental imagery', *Mind* 5: 301–18.

—— (1883) *Inquiries into Human Faculty and Its Development*, London: Macmillan.

—— (1884) 'On the anthropometric laboratory at the late International Health Exhibition', *Journal of the Anthropological Institute* 14: 205–21.

—— (1888) 'Co-relations and their measurement, chiefly from anthropometric data', *Proceedings of the Royal Society* 45: 135–45.

—— (1892) *Finger Prints*, London: Macmillan.

—— (1898) 'A diagram of heredity', *Nature* 57: 293.

—— (1908) *Memories of My Life*, London: Methuen.

—— (1909) *Essays in Eugenics*, London: Eugenics Education Society.

Gay, P. (1988) *Freud: A Life for our Time*, London: Dent.

Plate 2 William James (1842–1910)
By permission of Brown Brothers

2 William James (1842–1910)

Jerome L. Singer

William James was born in New York City to Mary Walsh and Henry James Sr in 1842. He was the first of their five children, four sons and a daughter. A year or so later, his brother, Henry, was born. Henry James Jr went on to become perhaps the greatest writer of novels and short fiction in America, author of The Portrait of a Lady, The Wings of a Dove, The Ambassadors, The Bostonians, The Turn of the Screw *and* The Aspern Papers, *among many others. Thus, Henry James Sr, the independently wealthy peripatetic writer of mystical and amorphous philosophical tracts, sired two of the giants of American intellectual history.*

William James went on to study both art and medicine, eventually taking his MD at Harvard University in 1869. Some extensive foreign travel in Europe and later a research expedition to Brazil with the famous Louis Agassiz preceded his completion of the degree. Although suffering through most of his life from physical ill health as well as periodic depressive periods, James rose steadily in scientific stature and academic rank at Harvard from 1869 to 1875. There he taught anatomy and physiology while also preparing himself in the then undefined field of psychology. The first course he taught in psychology was, as he quipped, the first he had ever taken.

James married in 1878, the same year he contracted to write The Principles of Psychology *for Henry Holt. He fathered five children while sustaining a hectic academic and research career. He conducted basic experimental research on the vestibular system and human motor activities and also pioneered the study of various forms of psychotherapy. As Harvard's first professor of psychology in 1889, he established a research laboratory, but soon passed this on to Hugo Munsterberg because he was becoming increasingly committed to philosophy. His work on pragmatism and on the nature of human will and intentionality, and his famous book* The

Varieties of Religious Experience, excited intellectuals all over the world.

In 1909, Sigmund Freud came to the United States to lecture on psychoanalysis at the request of the president of Clark University, G. Stanley Hall (once a student of James). Freud and James shared some extended private talks which were encouraging to the Viennese physician. Unfortunately, James died just a year later.

Defining William James' contribution is too restricting a task. In effect, he brought a clear-eyed and (in contrast to his father's mysticism) an open and healthy-minded directness to identifying an entire panoply of features of the human psychology that merited investigation. He wrote of habit as the 'great flywheel of society' and laid the foundations for learning theory. His work on emotions has challenged mind–body investigators for a century. His study of the nature of ongoing private thought first inspired a generation of great writers and fostered the literary genre of stream of consciousness that today is influential not only in novels and short stories but in scripts for film and television. Only more recently has this vein also been opened to mine the riches for psychological study that lie therein.

In his work on the self, James seemed far ahead of his time. It was not until the 1950s that psychologists recognized the potential value of studying the different representations of self which he had outlined as a basis for a large-scale research enterprise.

One can go on and on to explore the range of facets of the organism and, later in his philosophical work, of the existential challenges of will and intentionality which James first explored. He also proposed the notion of the 'moral equivalent of war', a conception of national and international service for youth that in America first came to fruition in 1961 as the Peace Corps. President Bill Clinton has proposed this concept as a basis for a national service corps.

It is just a little more than a century since William James published his monumental Principles of Psychology *(James 1952). Unlike the jazzy textbooks of today's post-television era with their multicoloured photographs, cartoons, clever boxes and low text-to-illustration ratio, James' two volumes of 689 pages each included only a few brain diagrams or sketches of optical illusions embedded in a vast proliferation of words. But what words! Rich in metaphors, daily life and clinical examples, reviews and critical analyses of practically all known philosophical and empirical research on mental science from America and Europe, this masterpiece of scholarship remains as exciting to read today as it must have been to the hardy souls who explored it one hundred years ago. Written in a clear and direct conversational style which contrasted with his brother's increasingly convoluted prose, the book led some to quip that William James was the better writer and Henry James the better psychologist.*

Such a comparison was certainly unfair to William, however. In this work he set forth, in his chapters on the brain, habit, consciousness, self, emotions, attention, perception and instinct, the agenda that prevails to this day for psychological research on neuroscience, motivation, emotion, learning, consciousness and social cognition. For over one hundred years, American psychologists have recognized William James as their premier and most distinguished psychologist. Indeed, he holds a comparable position as one of the United States' finest and most influential philosophers, a founder of pragmatism and of the functionalist orientation in intellectual thought. The American Psychological Association has sought for years to convince the United States Postal Service to recognize his importance through issuance of a postage stamp bearing his portrait. With a practicality that James would certainly have acknowledged by a bit of his dry humour, the Postal Service has recently moved much more rapidly to issue a stamp bearing the features of Elvis Presley: it sold out in one day.

To pursue all of the implications of James' thought would go far beyond what can be accomplished in one chapter. Instead I have chosen four areas in which James' ideas, somewhat neglected because of the behaviourist and animal research focus of psychology between 1910 and 1960, have been revived and have generated increasing research during the latter years of this century. These areas are: (1) the stream of thought, (2) the consciousness of self, (3) imagination and (4) the emotions. My approach will not be to summarize the proliferating research in these fields but rather to describe some fairly recent research[1] in which I personally have participated which may illustrate how vital to this day are the issues raised by William James. For more extended reviews of the implications of his life and work in psychology I call your attention to books, papers and monographs by Hilgard (1987), MacLeod (1969), Myers (1986), Natsoulas (1987, 1988, 1992) and Taylor (1983, 1992).

WILLIAM JAMES, JAMES JOYCE AND THE STREAM OF THOUGHT

What more fitting way to begin in Dublin than with James Joyce, who carried William James' great vision of those pulsations of thoughts that made up the stream of consciousness to their highest expression in literary art? The chapter on the stream of thought in James' *Principles* had been strategically placed very early in the text to highlight his emphasis on psychology as the study of mental life and of consciousness as the central feature of the human condition.

James' beautifully written and respected chapter on this topic had, however, little influence upon psychological research for almost seventy years. Perhaps this was because few methods for systematic study presented themselves and also because the huge rush towards animal research and 'objective' behaviourism precluded considering the phenomena of private experience as worthy of scientific psychological investigation. In this section I will address some recent relevant theory, research methods and findings that suggest ways in which current psychological research does address questions of awareness of one's own stream of conscious mentation. More detailed accounts of recent research are available elsewhere; here I will focus upon basic theory and some recent empirical studies (Singer and Kolligian 1987; Singer and Bonanno 1990).

I would like to begin with an example of the way the stream of consciousness operates. Here is a passage drawn from James Joyce's *Ulysses* because it encapsulates many of the issues that are of psychological interest while at the same time having the advantage of the poetic and dramatic beauty of which the greatest master of English prose of this century was capable. The interested reader can find comparable examples in psychologists' collections of streams of thought of 'real' people, available in Pope (1978) or Hurlburt (1990).

Early in *Ulysses* the young Irish would-be artist, Stephen Dedalus, gazes out of his window at the sea and then launches into a series of images, memories and interior monologues relating to the recent death of his mother. He recalls his refusal, despite her deathbed pleas, to return to the Catholic faith he had rejected and to pray for her:

> Woodshadows floated silently by through the morning peace from the stairhead seaward where he gazed. Inshore and farther out the mirror of water whitened, spurned by lightshod hurrying feet. White breast of the dim sea. The twining stresses, two by two. A hand plucking the harpstrings merging their twining chords. Wavewhite wedded words shimmering on the dim tide.
>
> A cloud began to cover the sun slowly, shadowing the bay in deeper green. It lay behind him, a bowl of bitter waters. Fergus' song: I sang it alone in the house, holding down the long dark chords. Her door was open: she wanted to hear my music. Silent with awe and pity I went to her bedside. She was crying in her wretched bed. For those words, Stephen: love's bitter mystery.
>
> Where now?
>
> Her secrets; old feather fans, tasselled dancecards, powdered with musk, a gaud of amber beads in her locked drawer. A birdcage hung in the sunny window of her house when she was a girl. . . . Memories beset his brooding brain. Her glass of water from the kitchen tap when she had approached the sacrament. A sacred apple, filled with brown sugar, roasting for her at the hob on a dark autumn evening. Her shapely fingernails reddened by the blood of squashed lice from the children's shirts.
>
> In a dream, silently, she had come to him, her wasted body within its loose graveclothes giving off an odour of wax and rosewood, her breath bent over him with mute secret words, a faint odour of wetted ashes.
>
> Her glazing eyes, staring out of death, to shake and bend my soul. On me alone. The ghostcandle to light her agony. Ghostly light on the tortured face. Her

hoarse loud breath rattling in horror, while all prayed
on their knees. Her eyes on me to strike me down. *Liliata
rutilantium te confessorum turma circumdet: iubilantium te
virginum chorus excipiat.*
Ghoul! Chewer of corpses!
No mother. Let me be and let me live.
(Joyce 1934: 11)

Let us now examine the passage from the standpoint of
modern psychological research on cognition and emotion.
The passage begins with essentially a perceptual experience,
albeit translated by the vocabulary of this highly literary
young man into Homeric metaphors of the waves and surf
lighted by a morning sun. The perceptual response then
shifts by an associative nexus to the words and, presumably, the melody of a song which Stephen sang to his
mother shortly before her death. Thereupon associations
become more remote from the direct perceptual experience;
images of the mother weeping in bed, beseeching him to
resume his faith, then of her private souvenirs of her youth
found in her bedroom, of early memories of her mother-
ing behaviour with her children, and then, from the deepest
consciousness, a memory of a dream in which his dead
mother appeared in her graveclothes, and then of her
deathbed while others in the family prayed on their knees.
The thought of him as a betrayer of the dead comes to mind
and then Stephen screams out mentally 'Let me be and let
me live', asserting in this way his rejection of the pressures
for attachment and communion with the others and insist-
ing on his autonomy and determination to develop his own
creative capacities.

Having first indulged his introspective and artistic
personal script (the shift from just looking to playing
with words and images), Stephen Dedalus becomes quickly
overwhelmed by images reflecting his conflict over need
for attachment, love of his mother and his family versus
his struggle for independent assertions, all played out in
thought. Then he must strive to control and direct the very
flood of images he had indulged initially.[2]

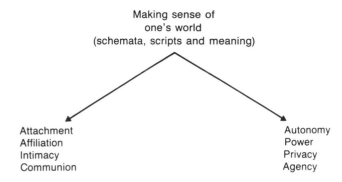

Making sense of
one's world
(schemata, scripts and meaning)

Attachment
Affiliation
Intimacy
Communion

Autonomy
Power
Privacy
Agency

Figure 2.1 The dominant psychological motives
Note: See also Singer and Bonanno 1990

This example points up sharply some issues I will raise in the balance of this chapter. As humans we must adapt ourselves continuously to shifting our attention between processing the external environment and noticing our ongoing thought stream, in which we first assimilate this new external information into established memory schemata and assign meanings (Kreitler and Kreitler 1976). We then become aware of memories or fantasies, possible future events or possible selves (Markus and Nurius 1986; Klinger 1990; Singer 1966, 1975), which we must somehow control and direct.

Modern cognitive psychology has shifted the emphasis away from the human being as driven by biological instincts of sex and aggression, a position of Freud's that held sway through the 1960s. Instead we see our motivation as first of all to make sense of the world and to organize new information into established cognitive schemata and mental scripts or verbal meanings and labels. Beneath this overarching need, as depicted in Figure 2.1, we can identify two continuing features of human motivation now widely agreed upon by developmental psychologists and personality theorists.

Humans struggle through each phase of their life span to reconcile the often competing pulls between, on the one hand, *attachment*, a desire for communion or for feeling oneself a part of some larger social, ethnic or religious unit, and, on the other, the need for *autonomy*, a sense of agency and personal fulfilment or expression of one's skills and capacities (Singer 1988a). A current formulation of the memory process, the shift between perceptual processing and the processing of material from the long-term memory system as well as the continuous reshaping of both new and old material has been proposed by Johnson (1990) and is exemplified in Figure 2.2, derived from Johnson and Multhaup (1992).

This model of memory, when combined with the more motivational emphasis exemplified in Figure 2.1, provides a way of understanding both the structure and content of the ongoing stream of thought. If we take a look again at Stephen Dedalus' consciousness in Joyce's example, we see how first he gazed idly at the sea, a purely perceptual reaction but one in which, beyond checking and noticing details and beginning labelling the experience (Johnson and Multhaup's P_1 and P_2 levels), he soon begins to fit the 'sea' imagery into a broader context of personal memory and to reflect (Johnson and Multhaup's R_1 and R_2) not just on the overarching cognitive motive but also on his need for closeness and attachment to his mother and family. This sense of warmth about belongingness, however, arouses another motive, his need to be independent, to assert both his intellectual powers (such as his denial of Catholic ritual) and also his powerful need for self-realization as an artist. This struggle is carried out privately and mentally so that an observer would notice only a young man leaning from the window of the apartment in the Martello tower, gazing seaward until his reverie is suddenly broken by being summoned to breakfast at the call of 'stately, plump Buck Mulligan'.

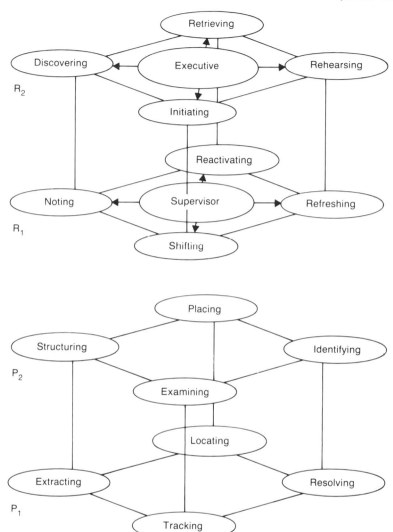

Figure 2.2 The components of a memory system
Source: Adapted from Johnson and Multhaup 1992

EMPIRICAL STUDIES OF DAYDREAMING AND THE STREAM OF THOUGHT

Our literary example, while it seems persuasive and can be understood now in the framework of the two models (the motivational and the cognitive, both themselves derived from empirical research), still leaves many technical questions for the scientific psychologist. One of our professional tasks, as James noted in his *Principles*, is to describe the range and variety of phenomena in a fashion that is precise, measurable and replicable by others. One must also seek to identify the *contingent* circumstances surrounding the emergence of a phenomenon such as the shift back and forth from perceptual consciousness.

Questionnaire studies

My own research in this field began when I sought to carry out some of the first empirical studies of normal adult daydreaming. This led first to a series of questionnaire studies and soon to one of experimental studies in which daydreams were recognized as a feature of the ongoing stream of consciousness. Singer and Antrobus (1972) developed a series of twenty-two scales of twelve items, each designed to measure a wide range of patterns of self-reported inner experience and types of daydream. This Imaginal Processes Inventory (IPI) has been factor-analysed in a number of different studies with varying samples across the age spectrum.

Briefly, a large number of studies indicate that most people report being aware of at least some daydreaming every day, and that their daydreams vary considerably from obvious wishful thinking of 'castles in Spain' to elaborate and complex visions of frightening or guilty encounters. Cultural differences in frequency and patterning of daydreaming as reported with these questionnaires also emerge. A series of factor-analytic studies indicate that, at least for the scales of the IPI, the data yield three major factors that characterize ongoing thought: (1) a positive-constructive daydreaming style, (2) a guilty-dysphoric daydreaming style, and (3) a poor attentional control pattern that is generally characterized by fleeting thoughts and an inability to focus on extended fantasy (Singer and Kolligian, 1987; Singer and Bonnano 1990). Giambra (1977a, 1977b) not only found evidence for factor patterns similar to those reported in these studies, but also tracked these across an extensive age range; in addition, he checked the test-retest reliability of daydreaming reports in response to this set of scales and found them to be surprisingly high.

Even with reliable and psychometrically well-constructed questionnaires we are still left with the issue of whether individual respondents can really summarize accurately their ongoing experiences, the frequency of particular daydreams, etc. Here we must turn to other estimates on ongoing thought or other forms of self-report to ascertain whether the questionnaire responses have some degree of validity. Reviewing such data, one finds that the self-reports obtained with questionnaires are correlated for the same respondents with:

1 daydream-like thoughts obtained during signal detection tasks;
2 vivid imaging to a point where objective external signals are undetected;
3 particular patterns of eye-shifts during reflective thought;
4 particular emphasis on analogy usage when language from thought samples is analysed;
5 particular forms of drug and alcohol use;
6 reported fantasies during sexual behaviour, daily recordings of dreams, hallucinations, flashbacks of traumatized veterans, hypnotic susceptibility, etc. (Singer and Bonanno 1990).

The proliferation of evidence from our own and related questionnaires suggests that the psychometric approach has considerable value in identifying individual stylistic variations in awareness and assignment of priorities to processing centrally generated information.

Laboratory studies of task-unrelated intrusive thought

My colleague John Antrobus and I developed a particular paradigm for attempting to estimate some parameters of ongoing thought. Using an approach that affords maximum 'control' over extraneous stimulation (at the cost of some artificiality or possibly reduced 'ecological validity'), we relied upon prolonged signal detection 'watches' by participants seated in soundproof, reduced-stimulation booths. Since the amount of external stimulation can be controlled, it remains to be determined to what extent individuals will shift their attention away from processing external cues (by which they earn money for accurate signal detection) towards the processing of material that is generated by the presumably ongoing activity of their own brains. Can we ascertain the conditions under which participants, even with high motivation for external signal processing, will still show evidence that they are carrying on task-unrelated intrusive thoughts (TUITs)?

Thus, if while detecting auditory signals an individual is interrupted (every 15 seconds) and questioned about whether any such task-unrelated thoughts occurred, a 'Yes' response is scored as a TUIT. If the participant and experimenter have agreed in advance on a common definition of what constitutes a task-irrelevant thought, the experimenter has at least some reasonable assurance that reports are more or less in keeping with the operational definition established. A thought such as 'Is that tone higher-pitched than the one before it? It sounded as if it was' is considered task-related and elicits a 'No' response, even though it is, of course, a thought. A response such as 'I've got to remember about picking up the car keys for my Saturday night date' is scored as a TUIT.

In this research paradigm, keeping the participants in booths for a fairly lengthy time and obtaining reports of the occurrence of task-unrelated intrusive thought after each 15 seconds of signal detection (with tones presented at rates of one per second) have made it possible to build up rather extensive information on the frequency of occurrence of

TUITs, as well as their relationship to the speed of signal presentation, the complexity of the task, and other characteristics of the subjects' psychological situation.

In addition to generalizations about the nature of cognitive processing (Singer 1988b), the signal detection model also permits the study of some individual differences in thought patterns. Antrobus *et al.* (1967) studied individuals already predisposed to be frequent daydreamers, according to their self-report. As time went on during their signal detection stay in the booth, such individuals were more likely to report TUITs than were participants who had reported on the questionnaire that they were little given to daydreaming.

Controlled studies of ongoing thought during signal detection 'watches' afford a rich opportunity for estimating the determinants of the thought stream. We know that the introduction of unusual or alarming information prior to entry into the detection booth (overhearing a broadcast of war news) can increase the amount of TUITs reported, even though accuracy of signal detections may not be greatly affected (Antrobus *et al.*, 1966).

Studies using auditory and visual signal detection or vigilance models with interruptions for reports have also made it possible to ascertain that reports of TUITs occur more than 50 per cent of the time even when subjects are attaining very high detection rates, when signals come as frequently as every 0.5 seconds and when density of signal information is increased. Indeed, it was possible to show evidence for not only sequential but also parallel processing of the TUITs and the external signals. When external signals were visual (such as lights), visual content of TUITs was reduced relative to verbal content. The effect was reversed when external signals were auditory. This result suggests that our daydream processes in particular modalities of sensory imagery use the same brain pathways as are needed for processing external cues. Other studies of continuous talk in these laboratory settings point to the moderately arousing, vigilance-maintaining quality of ongoing thought and also to the dependence of such thought on factors such as physical posture and the social setting. For example, when experimenters and participants are of the opposite sex there is a significant increase in TUIT reports during signal detections (Singer 1988b; Singer and Bonanno 1990).

Thought sampling in more 'natural' circumstances

Some methods that sacrifice the rigid controls of the signal detection booth for greater ecological relevance have been increasingly employed in the development of an approach to determining the characteristics and determinants of waking conscious thought. These involve (1) asking participants to talk out loud over a period of time while in a controlled environment, with the scoring of such verbalization along empirically or theoretically derived categories; (2) allowing the respondent to sit, recline or stand quietly for a period of time and interrupting the person periodically for reports of thought or perceptual activity; or (3) requiring the person to signal by means of a button press whenever a new chain of thought begins, and then to report verbally in retrospect or to fill out a prepared rating form characterizing various possible features of ongoing thought.

The use of thought sampling in a reasonably controlled environment also permits evaluation of a variety of conditions that may influence or characterize ongoing consciousness. One can score the participants' verbalizations on dimensions such as (1) organized, sequential versus degenerative, confused thought; (2) use of imagery, related episodes or event memory material versus logical-semantic structures; (3) reference to current concerns and unfulfilled intentions; (4) reminiscence of past events versus orientation toward the future; and (5) realistic versus improbable content.

Two studies of my students may be cited here. Pope (1978) demonstrated that longer sequences of thought with more remoteness from the participants' immediate circumstances were obtained when the respondents were reclining rather than walking freely and when they were alone rather than in an interpersonal situation. Zachery (1983) evaluated the relative role of positive and negative emotional experiences just prior to the thought-sampling period. He found that intensity of experience rather than its emotional valence and, to a lesser extent, the relative ambiguity versus clarity of the material determined recurrence in the thought stream.

Other research points to the relative importance of current concerns as determinants of the material that merges in thought sampling. 'Current concerns' are defined as a state between the times when one becomes committed to pursuing a particular goal and when one either consummates or abandons this objective (Klinger 1990). In estimating current concerns at a point in time prior to thought-sampling sessions, one obtains scale estimates of the valences of the goals, the relative importance of intentions in some value and temporal hierarchy, the person's perception of the reality of goal achievement, and so on. It seems clear that only after we have explored the range and influence of such current, consciously unfulfilled intentions in a sampling of the individual's thoughts, emotions and behavioural responses can we move to infer the influence of unconscious wishes or intentions.

The past decade has reflected a considerable interest in thought-sampling studies that move outside the laboratory. Research now involves an accumulation of data over as much as two weeks, during which participants carrying paging devices ('beepers') report on their thoughts, emotions and current activities when signalled several times a day (Csikszentmihalyi and Larson 1984; Hurlburt 1990; Klinger 1990). Data suggest the feasibility of this method and its suitability for hypothesis testing as well as for accumulating basic descriptive data (as in the Csikszentmihalyi and Larson study of teenagers).

An example of this approach is found in a study where participants' prior fantasies of intimacy were measured. It was found that those with higher motivation for establishing close relationships actually reported more interpersonal thoughts and more positive emotional responses in interpersonal situations in their sampled reports than did low-intimacy-motive scorers. These data were based on a week-long accumulation of eight daily reports (McAdams and Constantian 1983).

The accumulation of thought samples has also proved useful in studies of clinical groups such as bulimics or panic disorder patients, where the time, locale and contingent circumstances associated with recurrent thoughts have yielded meaningful data (Singer and Bonanno 1990). In individual case studies, I have found that samples of the ongoing conscious thought of normal individuals include many of the metaphors or symbols that these people also reported when recounting subsequent night dreams. The prior days' ongoing consciousness seemed to include images or phrases that were already laying the groundwork for what appear to be the strange or creative symbols of the night dream.

MANIFESTATIONS OF SELF AND THEIR RELATION TO EMOTION

William James followed his discussion of the thought stream with a chapter on consciousness of self and, later on in the book, with one on emotion. In Stephen's interior monologue we saw all these elements converge as his associations led to a delineation first of his mother, then of an awareness of his own role and personal needs. Along with this content he seemed to be experiencing emotions of wistful melancholy, guilt, terror (the dream of his dead mother in her graveclothes), guilt again, and finally defiant anger. Let me describe some recent research that addresses the interrelations of ongoing thought, experiences of self and specific emotional arousal.

Determinants of the content of ongoing thought

An approach using a natural thought-sampling procedure may next be described. Here we set up a hierarchy of possible conditions that might lead events or emotions experienced in an experimental situation to recur when later thoughts were sampled after the experimental intervention. Our participants were a group of adolescents. By having the thought reports rated by trained judges for their similarity or dissimilarity to the particular experimental scenarios experienced by our subjects (the judges were of course blind to the experimental conditions), we could estimate whether particular kinds of experience are more or less conducive to yielding recurrences in the later thought stream of the individual (Klos and Singer 1981).

In this study, a hierarchy of experimental conditions was set up prior to a thought-sampling procedure. These situations were expected to yield differential degrees of recurrence in the consciousness of the participants. It was proposed that even for beginning college students, simulated parental involvements were likely to prove especially provocative of further thought. We chose to evaluate the relative recurrence in later thought of:

1 resolved versus unresolved situations (the old Zeigarnick effect);
2 a mutual problem-solving but non-conflictual parental interaction;
3 a confrontation or conflict with a parent that involved either a collaborative stance by the adult; or
4 a comparable confrontation in which the parent's attitude was clearly coercive rather than collaborative.

It was proposed that exposure (through a simulated interaction) to each of these conditions would yield differences in the later recurrence of simulation-relevant thoughts in the participants' consciousness. Specifically, we anticipated that unresolved situations and particularly those involving confrontation would be most likely to be reflected in the post-experimental thought streams of our participants.

The data provided clear support for the major hypotheses. The frequency of thought recurrences occurred in

38 *Jerome L. Singer*

the predicted order. The effects were strongly amplified by an actual history of long-standing interpersonal stress with a parent. The pure incompletion effect was a modest one, mainly in evidence in the non-conflictual situation. It was overridden by the increasing coerciveness of the imaginary conflict situations. Of special interest is the fact that, once exposed to a simulated conflict with a parent, young people with a history of stress reflected this brief, artificial incident in as many as 50 per cent of their later sampled thoughts (Figure 2.3). If we tentatively generalize from these results, the thought-world of adolescents who have had long-standing parental difficulties may be a most unpleasant domain, since many conflictual chance encounters or even

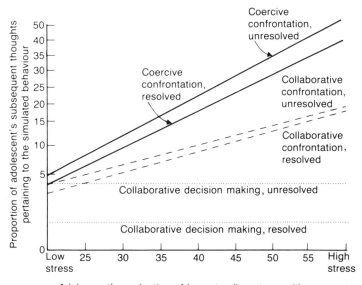

Adolescent's evaluation of long-standing stress with a parent

Figure 2.3 Interactive effects of simulated parental confrontation and long-standing stress with a parent on post-simulation thought
Source: Klos and Singer 1981
Note: The interaction of confrontation and long-standing interpersonal stress is reflected in the proportion of the subject's thoughts about the simulated parental confrontation during a twenty-minute period following the experiment. Note that unresolved confrontations produce a higher proportion of thoughts.

film or television plots may lead to a considerable degree of associative thought recurrence. Stephen Dedalus' association of the lapping waters with harpstrings and Fergus' song is sufficient to produce a parental association and to change his mood from one of calm appreciation of scenic beauty to one of inner torment. The implications of a method of the kind described (combined with estimates of personality variables or of other current concerns) for studying various groups (e.g. clinical patients, post-surgical patients, hypertensives) seem very intriguing.

Self-belief discrepancies in cocaine abusers

A special insight which William James provided (but which was largely overlooked for many years) was his proposal that it is vain to search for a 'true or unique self'. Instead we hold multiple beliefs about ourselves related to ideal selves, selves in specific settings, past or future selves. The past decade in psychology has shown an impressive upsurge in interest in how such self-beliefs in their various manifestations may guide or disrupt our behaviour or may actually evoke specific emotional responses.

Recently S. Kelly Avants, Arthur Margolin, William Kosten and I sought to test hypotheses derived from the work of Tory Higgins on the linkage between self-belief discrepancies and specific affective states. Higgins (1987) had proposed that we all formulate a series of self-beliefs which can be about our actual selves, our ideal selves, our ought selves (selves that we believe our significant others expect of us) and other kinds of self-representation such as past, future and dreaded self. Higgins had shown that measured large discrepancies between actual self and ideal self were likely to lead to depression or sadness, while discrepancies between actual self and ought self might lead more to agitation, anxiety and fearful emotions. On the premise that cocaine abusers may be self-medicating a depressive mood by using an 'uplifting' drug, we hypothesized that this class of abusers should show more evidence of an actual self–ideal self discrepancy than either a heroin-use group or a non-abusing control.

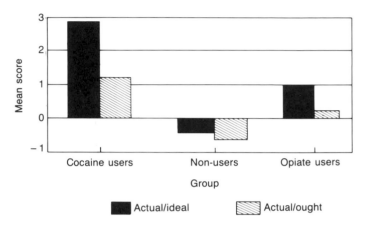

Figure 2.4 Self-discrepancy scores for cocaine users, non-users and opiate users
Source: Avants, Singer and Margolin 1993

Our data in Figure 2.4 clearly support this hypothesis. Thought samples of the participants were also employed and we could show how cravings for cocaine emerged along with reports of greater actual–ideal discrepancies on a day-to-day basis. We then moved on to actual psychological treatment of these patients by having them keep logs of their moods and of their thoughts of self as 'addict', 'ideal', 'craving', etc. while a cognitive-behavioural therapy intervention sought to help them identify and practise more adaptive self-representations. Follow-up thought samples revealed correlations between less craving, less actual–ideal discrepancies, more positive future selves, less craving in the face of drug cues, and greater physiologically measured abstinence (Avants *et al.* 1993).

Manifestations of self, emotions and ongoing thought

Another approach to relating self-beliefs, emotions and thought samples with over 100 normal young adults has recently been attempted in a collaboration of Daniel Hart, Nigel Field, Jonathan Garfinkle, Karen Anderson and myself. Following up the work on discrepancies between actual self, ideal self, dreaded self, etc., and the arousal of specific emotions such as depression or agitation, we have first tested these participants on a variety of major personality dimensions, including neuroticism, extraversion, conscientiousness, openness-imaginativeness and amiability, as well as on measures of depression and anxiety. We also measured at length the participants' descriptions of significant others and of their various selves (actual, ideal, dreaded, past, future) on self-generated adjective scales. We also followed them for over a week while they carried paging devices timed to go off randomly eight times daily. At each signal they filled out sheets describing their moods, specific thoughts and contingent activities.

We are still analysing the data for measures of content and for tests of specific hypotheses for the built-in experiments in the study. Some results are available, however. First of all we again confirmed the theory of Higgins that indicates that the large actual self–ideal self discrepancy (meaning that a person's current self-appraisal is far removed from his or her ideal) is associated with a depressive mood, not only on personality tests but also when we accumulate the dozens of reported emotions obtained when sampling the participants' streams of thought over a week. Such a notion was already foreshadowed in a simple diagram on page 310 of James' *Principles*, volume 1. In addition we can show that particular fluctuations in ideal, actual and dreaded self may be associated with the relative activity level and degree of emotional arousal reflected in the participants' thought streams. What is particularly important in the light of James' original emphasis on multiple selves is that discrepancies between the various manifestations of self are excellent predictors in multiple regression analyses in the hypothesized direction. Thus the actual–ought discrepancy was the best predictor of anxiety, as Higgins (1987) had proposed, and the actual–undesirable (or dreaded) self discrepancy was important in predicting levels of self-esteem (Hart *et al.* in preparation).

A COGNITIVE-AFFECTIVE PERSPECTIVE

I should like to close by summarizing my conclusions from years of applying these methods to studying ongoing thought. I propose that human beings are best regarded as creatures who are biologically endowed with the necessary capacities and who are motivated from birth to explore their environments and to move gradually towards labelling and assigning meaning to their experiences. The human information-processing systems are closely tied to the separate, differentiated affective system, so that we are aroused, frightened, angered or depressed by large degrees of sudden or persisting incongruity between our expectancies (plans, goals or wishes) and the information presented in a given situation. Likewise, we are moved to laughter and joy when incongruities are resolved, or to interest and to exploration when the novelty we confront is at a moderate level rather than an extreme one (Mandler 1984; Singer 1974, 1984; Tomkins 1962–3).

If we are indeed 'wired' to make sense of our environment – to select, to identify, to label, to encode and to schematize new stimulation – what are the sources of this information? For human beings (as far as we can tell) our stimuli derive either from the 'objective' world, the consensually measurable physical and social stimuli in our milieu, or from the 'subjective' or private world of our memories and ongoing mental processes (Pope and Singer 1978). At any given moment the human being must assign a priority to responding either to those stimuli that come from exodermic sources (sounds, light patterns, smells, touches or tastes) or to those that appear to be 'internal' (the recollections, associations, images, interior monologues, wishful

fantasies or ruminative worries that characterize consciousness). Bodily sensations or signals, or pain or malfunction
from our organ systems, represent a kind of intermediate
source of stimulation, although such experiences often
appear to us to have an 'objective' quality, despite their
inherent embeddedness within our physical selves. We
must generally give greater weight in our instantaneous
assignments of priority to externally derived stimuli, or else
we are likely to be hit by cars, to bump into poles, or to
step into ditches. But human environments are characterized by sufficient redundancy, and our motor skills and
cognitive plans for specific situations generally are so
overlearned and well differentiated that we have ample
opportunity to engage in elaborate memories, planful
thought or fantasies even while driving cars or participating
in business meetings.

Our human condition is such that we are forever in the
situation of deciding how much attention to give to self-
generated thought and how much to information from the
external social and physical environment. The conflict
between processing external and reflective information is
one manifestation of, or perhaps even is the prototype for,
the major existential dilemma of the human being – the
persisting dialectical struggle between autonomy and affiliation. Beneath the umbrella of the overarching motive for
meaning, we humans are always seeking, on the one hand,
to be part of someone or some system beyond ourselves
– to feel loved, admired or respected, to feel close to an
individual or a group – and, on the other, to sustain a sense
of autonomy and individuality, or self-direction, privacy
in thought, or uniqueness in competence and skill. The
individual stream of consciousness, as William James seems
to suggest, may be conceived as the human's last bastion
of privacy and sense of uniqueness. Yet our studies of ongoing consciousness point out that a great majority of our
thoughts are about affiliation and attachment to others.

We return at last to our two protagonists, William James,
who identified the stream of consciousness as a central
psychological phenomenon, and James Joyce, who put it

to artistic uses. The self-exiled Dubliner, in his wonderful literary exemplifications of the thought stream of his alter ego, Stephen, demonstrates subtly and, perhaps, not entirely consciously how the young hero, even as he asserts his independence, is yet driven towards communion 'to forge in the smithy of my soul the uncreated conscience of my race'. So, too, James Joyce, the independent old artificer, sat in far-off Trieste or Zurich asserting his autonomy through his writing. But in his stream of consciousness his thoughts were ever with his family, his friends and acquaintances, and the never-forgotten streets of his beloved Dublin.

NOTES

1   Some of the most recent research by the author which is cited herein was supported by a grant to the Program on Conscious and Unconscious Mental Processes at the University of California, San Francisco, from the John D. and Catherine T. MacArthur Foundation.
2   For a literary analysis of this and other passages from *Ulysses*, see Steinberg (1973).

REFERENCES

Antrobus, J.S., Coleman, R. and Singer, J.L. (1967) 'Signal detection performance by subjects differing in predisposition to daydreaming', *Journal of Consulting Psychology* 31: 487–91.
Antrobus, J.S., Singer, J.L. and Greenberg, S. (1966) 'Studies in the stream of consciousness: experimental enhancement and suppression of spontaneous cognitive processes', *Perceptual and Motor Skills* 23: 399–417.
Avants, S.K., Singer, J.L. and Margolin, A. (1993) 'Self-representations and negative affect in cocaine-dependent individuals', *Imagination, Cognition and Personality* 13: 3–24.
Csikszentmihalyi, M. and Larson, R. (1984) *Being Adolescent*, New York: Basic Books.
Giambra, L.M. (1977a) 'Adult male daydreaming across the life span: a replication, further analyses, and tentative norms based upon retrospective reports', *International Journal of Aging and Human Development* 8: 197–228.
—— (1977b) 'Daydreaming about the past: the time setting of spontaneous thought intrusions', *The Gerontologist* 17(a): 35–8.
Hart, D., Feld, N., Garfinkle, J., Singer, J.L. and Anderson, K. (in

preparation) 'Representations of self and other: relations to personality, mood and emotions'.

Higgins, E.T. (1987) 'Self-discrepancy: a theory relating self and affect', *Review* 94: 319–40.

Hilgard, E. (1987) *Psychology in America*, San Diego, CA: Harcourt Brace Jovanovich.

Hurlburt, R.T. (1990) *Sampling Normal and Schizophrenic Inner Experience*, New York: Plenum.

James, W. (1952) *The Principles of Psychology*, 2 vols, New York: Dover. (Original work published 1890.)

Johnson, M.K. (1990) 'Functional forms of human memory', in J.L. McGaugh, N.M. Winberger and G. Lynch (eds) *Brain Organization and Memory: Cells, Systems and Circuits*, New York: Oxford University Press.

Johnson, M.K. and Multhaup, K. (1992) 'Emotion and MEM', in S.A. Christianson (ed.) *Handbook of Emotion and Memory*, Hillsdale, NJ: Erlbaum.

Joyce, J. (1934) *Ulysses*, New York: Random House.

Klinger, E. (1990) *Daydreaming*, Los Angeles: Tarcher.

Klos, D.S. and Singer, J.L. (1981) 'Determinants of the adolescent's ongoing thought following simulated parental confrontations', *Journal of Personality and Social Psychology* 41: 975–87.

Kreitler, H. and Kreitler, S. (1976) *Cognitive Orientation and Behavior*, New York: Springer-Verlag.

McAdams, D. and Constantian, C.A. (1983) 'Intimacy and affiliation motives in daily living: an experience sampling analysis', *Journal of Personal and Social Psychology* 4: 851–61.

MacLeod, R. (ed.) (1969) *William James: Unfinished Business*, Washington, DC: American Psychological Association.

Mandler, G. (1984) *Mind and Body*, New York: Norton.

Markus, H. and Nurius, P. (1986) 'Possible selves', *American Psychologist* 41: 954–69.

Myers, G.E. (1986) *William James: His Life and Thought*, New Haven, CT: Yale University Press.

Natsoulas, T. (1987) 'Gibson, James and the temporal continuity of experience', *Imagination, Cognition and Personality* 7: 351–76.

—— (1988) 'Understanding William James's conception of consciousness with the help of Gerald E. Myers', *Imagination, Cognition and Personality* 8: 323–44.

—— (1992) 'The stream of consciousness: William James's pulses', *Imagination, Cognition and Personality* 12: 3–22.

Pope, K.S. (1978) 'How gender, solitude and posture influence the stream of consciousness', in K.S. Pope and J.L. Singer (eds) *The Stream of Consciousness*, New York: Plenum.

Pope, K.S. and Singer, J.L. (1978) 'Regulation of the stream of consciousness: toward a theory of ongoing thought', in G.E. Schwartz and D. Shapiro (eds) *Consciousness and Self-regulation. Vol. 2*, New York: Plenum.

Singer, J.L. (1966) *Daydreaming*, New York: Random House.

—— (1974) *Imagery and Daydream Methods in Psychotherapy and Behavior*

46 *Jerome L. Singer*

Modification, New York: Academic Press.
—— (1975) 'Navigating the stream of consciousness: research in daydreaming and related inner experience', *American Psychologist* 30: 727–38.
—— (1984) *The Human Personality*, New York and San Diego: Harcourt Brace Jovanovich.
—— (1988a) 'Psychoanalytic theory in the context of contemporary psychology', *Psychoanalytic Psychology* 5: 95–125.
—— (1988b) 'Sampling ongoing consciousness and emotional experience: implications for health', in M.J. Horowitz (ed.) *Psychodynamics and Cognition*, Chicago: University of Chicago Press.
Singer, J.L. and Antrobus, J.S. (1972) 'Daydreaming, imaginal processes, and personality: a normative study', in P. Sheehan (ed.) *The Function and Nature of Imagery*, New York: Academic Press.
Singer, J.L. and Bonanno, G.A. (1990) 'Personality and private experience: individual variations in consciousness and in attention to subjective phenomena', in L. Pervin (ed.) *Handbook of Personality: Theory and Research*, New York: Guilford Press.
Singer, J.L. and Kolligian, J., Jr (1987) 'Personality: developments in the study of private experience', *Annual Review of Psychology* 38: 533–74.
Steinberg, E.R. (1973) *The Stream of Consciousness and Beyond in Ulysses*, Pittsburgh, PA: University of Pittsburgh Press.
Taylor, E. (1983) *William James on Exceptional Mental States*, New York: Scribners.
—— (1992) 'William James's contribution to experimental psychology', *History of Psychology Newsletter*, XXIV: 3–6.
Tomkins, S.S. (1962–3) *Affect, Imagery, Consciousness*, 2 vols, New York: Springer.
Zachery, R. (1983) 'Cognitive and affective determinants of ongoing thought', unpublished doctoral dissertation, Yale University.

Plate 3 Sigmund Freud (1856–1939)
By permission of Mary Evans Picture Library

3 Sigmund Freud (1856–1939)

Anthony Storr

Sigmund Freud was born on 6 May 1856 in the Moravian town of Freiberg, now Pribor in the Czech Republic. His mother Amalie was the third wife of Jacob Freud, a Jewish wool merchant, some twenty years younger than her husband. In 1859, when Sigmund Freud was 3 years old, the family moved to Vienna. For the next seventy-nine years Freud continued to live and work in this city, for which he recurrently professed distaste, but which he was extremely reluctant to leave. At the age of 67, he developed a cancerous condition of the palate which recurred throughout the remainder of his life, requiring more than thirty operations. In 1938, he was compelled to take refuge from the Nazis, and spent the last year of his life in England, dying on 23 September 1939, shortly after the beginning of the Second World War.

Freud enrolled in the medical department of the University of Vienna in the autumn of 1873, but did not graduate until 30 March 1881. His initial interest was in zoological research. From 1876 to 1882 he carried out research in the Physiological Institute of Ernst Brücke, an authority whom he greatly admired and who exercised a considerable influence upon his thinking. Brücke and his co-workers were dedicated to the idea, then not widely accepted, that all vital processes could ultimately be explained in terms of physics and chemistry, thus eliminating religious and vitalist concepts from biology. Freud remained a determinist throughout his life; believing that all vital phenomena, including psychological phenomena like thoughts, feelings and phantasies, are rigidly determined by the principle of cause and effect.

Freud was reluctant to practise medicine, and would have preferred to spend his life in research. But in 1882 he fell in love with Martha Bernays. Since there was no possibility of his earning enough to support a wife and family if he remained in Brücke's laboratory,

Freud gave up research and spent the next three years studying in the Vienna general hospital in order to be able to embark upon medical practice. In 1885 he was appointed a lecturer in neuropathology at the University of Vienna. From October 1885 to February 1886 he studied at the Salpêtière Hospital in Paris under Charcot, the great neurologist who had made a special study of hysteria. Charcot stimulated Freud's interest in the problems of neurosis, as opposed to organic diseases of the nervous system. On his return from Paris, Freud embarked upon medical practice in Vienna, and was finally able to marry his fiancée in September 1886.

Their first child was born in October 1887. Five more children followed, the last being Anna Freud, who was born in 1895. She was the only one of Freud's children to become a psychoanalyst. Although his wife Martha devoted herself entirely to Freud's welfare and that of the children, as befitted a Victorian wife, she showed little appreciation of his work. Anna became his confidante and close collaborator, and devotedly cared for him in his terminal illness. But Martha provided a background of tranquillity which relieved him from the commonplace tasks of everyday life, and although we know from letters that their sexual relationship declined comparatively early, he could not have achieved so much if his marriage had not been so harmonious.

From the mid-1890s onward, Freud's life becomes the history of the development of psychoanalysis. 'Studies on hysteria', written jointly with Josef Breuer, appeared in 1895. If one considers the influence which Freud has had upon contemporary thought and the fact that his own contributions to psychoanalysis are so extensive as to require twenty-four volumes, it is extraordinary that the first psychoanalytic publication did not appear until he was 39 years old. Freud claimed that, for him, the creative imagination and work went together. He was an enormously productive writer.

Freud had a lively appreciation of literature. The excellence of his own literary style was recognized when he was still a schoolboy. In 1930, he became the fourth recipient of the Goethe prize for literature awarded by the City of Frankfurt. In Freud's collected works there are more references to Goethe and to Shakespeare than there are to the writings of any psychiatrist. He collected antiquities, and appreciated sculpture and painting, but had no ear for music. His personality can be described as obsessional: that is, he was a compulsive worker; orderly, scrupulous and obstinate.

Freud's inhibited, controlled nature extended to his autobiography, which concentrates almost entirely upon the development of psychoanalysis and tells us next to nothing about his personal life. As early as 1885, he wrote to his fiancée telling her that he had destroyed his notes, letters and manuscripts of the last fourteen years, presciently adding that he had no desire to make it easy for his future biographers. Freud, the man who spent his life investigating the kinds of intimate secrets which people strive to conceal from themselves as well as from others, was extremely reluctant to reveal his own.

FREUD REVISITED

Freud, Darwin and Marx are often linked as the three original thinkers who have most altered people's view of themselves in the twentieth century. Freud's ideas have exerted so powerful an influence that, in Western countries, psychoanalysis has become the most widely accepted idiom for discussing personality and interpersonal relationships. When I was young, psychiatrists were either Freudians or they were not. To be a Freudian implied having been through the process of Freudian analysis and also assumed acceptance of the greater part of what Freud had written as being true in the scientific sense. However, even amongst the Freudian establishment, some of Freud's ideas, particularly the concept of the death instinct, were disputable. It was recognized that Freud's notions about women rested upon outmoded nineteenth-century attitudes; and a number of psychoanalysts were uneasy about his 'armchair' anthropology. But the broad outline of Freud's psychoanalytic theoretical scheme was wholeheartedly embraced by analysts and analysands; and anyone who seriously questioned it was regarded as ignorant, misguided, or so neurotic as to be manifesting impenetrable resistance.

During the last forty years, this position has changed. There are still a few Freudian analysts who can justly be described as fundamentalists; who believe that psychoanalysis in its original form is the only kind of psychotherapy worth pursuing. Analysts of this kind have such an unquestioning faith in psychoanalysis as a treatment that, if it is unsuccessful, they blame the patient rather than the method for their failure to help him or her. I can recall a book on the training of psychiatrists in which a young resident was reported as saying: 'The wonderful thing about psychoanalysis is that, even if the patient doesn't get better, you know you are doing the right thing.' Freud died over fifty years ago on 23 September 1939. It is now possible to assess his contributions objectively, without being accused either of misunderstanding them or of undue partisanship. Since being commissioned by the Oxford University Press to write a short book on Freud, I have re-read a good deal of his writings, albeit in the James Strachey translation, rather than in the original German. Two things particularly impressed me.

The first is the clarity and persuasiveness of Freud's style. No wonder the City of Frankfurt awarded him the Goethe prize for literature. Even in translation, Freud is a pleasure to read. When an author combines persuasiveness with elegance of style and an absolute conviction of his own rightness, it is hard to resist him. I am sure that Freud's skill as a writer partly accounts for the widespread influence of his doctrines throughout the Western world.

The second thing which impressed me is the sheer bulk of his writings. From his schooldays onward, Freud was always a hard worker. During his years as a research worker in the laboratories of Ernst Brücke, he produced a number of papers on neurophysiology, and later wrote a mono-graph on aphasia. But the first psychoanalytic publication, 'Studies on hysteria', written jointly with Breuer, did not appear until 1895, the year in which Freud attained the age of 39. Yet his psychoanalytical works alone, excluding the book of indexes, require twenty-three volumes in the Standard Edition. Freud lived until the age of 83; but we have to remember that the last sixteen years of his life were marred by a cancer of his palate which required more than thirty operations. I wonder if there is any other example of a man of genius only starting on his true path so late in life and yet, in spite of illness, producing such a huge quantity of original work?

What kind of personality is able to achieve so much within the span of only half a lifetime? Many people of outstanding intellectual achievement display obsessional traits of personality, and Freud was no exception. He himself recognized this, and told Jung that, if he were to suffer from neurosis, it would be of obsessional type. Freud, in his paper of 1913, 'The disposition to obsessional neurosis', described the intellectual precocity which so often occurs in intelligent obsessionals. When at school, Freud was first in his class for six successive years. He began to read Shakespeare at the age of 8. By the time he left school, he had a thorough knowledge of Greek, Latin, French and English as well as of his native German. He also learned Hebrew, and taught himself the rudiments of Spanish and Italian. Goethe and Shakespeare remained his favourite authors. Freud combined dedication to work with his intellectual precocity. He wrote to his friend Fliess that he needed a 'dominating passion', and claimed that he could not contemplate a life without work. Although Freud usually took a long summer vacation during which he was an energetic walker, he allowed himself little time for relaxation during the week. Most of his writing was done on Sundays, or late at night after a day in which he might have spent eight or nine demanding hours seeing analytic patients.

Freud exhibited all the most valuable traits which are found in the obsessional personality. He was scrupulous, self-controlled and passionately concerned with the pursuit of truth. Although early poverty must have made it difficult, Freud was always neat in his dress and appearance. A barber attended him daily to trim his hair and beard. Freud described obsessional personalities as being especially *orderly*, *parsimonious* and *obstinate*. He himself was certainly orderly and obstinate. He may have appeared parsimonious in his early days, when he was poor and dependent on the financial help of friends. His own tastes remained simple, and he never owned more than three sets of clothes. In later years, he could not tolerate owing money and, although charging high fees to those who could afford them, gave generous financial help to those in need, including some patients, his own relatives and penurious students.

He also suffered from some of the negative traits so often found in obsessional personalities. He was superstitious about numbers. For many years, he was convinced that he would die between the ages of 61 and 62. He thought it uncanny that the numbers 61 and 60 kept cropping up in connection with the numbers 1 or 2. Thus, he believed it significant when he was assigned a hotel room with the number 31; that is, half of 62. In the year in which he became 43, he received a new telephone number, 14362. It seemed to him plausible to assume that the digits 1, 6 and 2, in association with 43, signified the end of his life.

His smoking was certainly compulsive. During the years 1893–6, he suffered from a cardiac arrhythmia which was attributable to smoking, but he could not abstain for long. Although he knew that smoking was an agent contributing to the cancer of the palate which plagued his declining years, he was still unable to give up the cigars which brought him so much solace.

His collecting habits were characteristically obsessional. Freud had a passion for antiquities, and avidly collected Greek, Roman and Etruscan statuettes, even during the early part of his life when he could ill afford them. Photographs of his apartment in Vienna, and the later reconstruction of that apartment at 20 Maresfield Gardens, now the Freud Museum in London, show these objects crowding the bookshelves and the top of Freud's desk so closely that no single one can be appreciated as a work of art in its own right. This agglomeration is not that of a connoisseur but that of an obsessional collector whose interest is in accumulation rather than in beauty.

Although Freud himself made major modifications to psychoanalytic theory during the course of his long life, virtually no one else was allowed to do so. His intolerance toward those who questioned his ideas bore witness to his rigidity. Freud's passionate conviction that he was right contributed to his charismatic powers of persuasion, but, when combined with his inflexibility, led to the series of defections which so disfigure the early history of the psychoanalytic movement. Amongst the more important rebels were Alfred Adler, Wilhelm Stekel, Carl G. Jung and Otto Rank.

I think it legitimate to point out that some of the basic features of psychoanalytic theory can be attributed to Freud's obsessional personality. Freud was essentially a dualist who habitually explained mental phenomena in terms of the interaction of, or conflict between, opposites. When Freud revised psychoanalytic theory after the First World War, he proposed a dualistic scheme in which all the phenomena of mental life could ultimately be traced to the interaction of two drives.

> After long hesitations and vacillations we have decided to assume the existence of only two basic instincts, *Eros* and the *destructive instinct*.... The aim of the first of these basic instincts is to establish ever greater unities and to preserve them thus – in short, to bind together; the aim of the second is, on the contrary, to undo connections and to destroy things. In the case of the destructive instinct we may suppose that its final aim is to lead what is living into an inorganic state. For this reason we also call it *the death instinct*.
>
> (Freud 1964: 148)

There is no obvious reason other than Freud's personal dualistic preference for limiting human instincts to two. For example, sleep and eating are largely determined by innate needs. But Freud not only needed a dualistic scheme; he needed one which appeared to be all-embracing. It is characteristic of obsessional personalities to wish to control as many aspects of life as possible. Many compulsive rituals, especially those connected with cleanliness and orderliness, can be traced to the obsessional's anxiety that, unless he or she takes especial pains, things will get out of hand and end in chaos. Hence, obsessionals are particularly attracted by views of the world and of human nature which are sufficiently all-embracing to promise, if not total control, at least total understanding. Freud ultimately concluded that the whole of civilization, and hence all that is characteristically human, including neurosis, can be understood in terms of a perpetual struggle between Eros and the death instinct. It is a majestic vision. Freud pictures civilization as

> a process in the service of Eros, whose purpose is to combine single human individuals, and after that families, then races, peoples and nations, into one great unity, the unity of mankind.... But man's natural aggressive instinct, the hostility of each against all and all against each, oppose this programme of civilization. This aggressive instinct is the derivative and the main representative of the death instinct which we have found alongside of Eros and which shares world-dominion with it. And now, I think, the meaning of the evolution of civilization is no longer obscure to us. It must present the struggle between Eros and Death, between the instinct of life and the instinct of destruction as it works itself out in the human species. This struggle is what all life essentially consists of, and the evolution of civilization may therefore be simply described as the struggle for life of the human species. And it is this battle of giants that our nurse-maids try to appease with their lullaby about Heaven.
>
> (Freud 1961a: 122)

This quotation from one of Freud's later works, *Civilization and Its Discontents*, illustrates his belief that civilization, although necessary for human survival as a species, was nevertheless a terrible burden which, as he put it, inflicts 'injuries' upon the individual. In an ironic passage from *The Future of an Illusion*, Freud reveals what he thought would happen if the natural man cast away his chains.

We have spoken of the hostility to civilization which is produced by the pressure that civilization exercises, the renunciation of instinct which it demands. If one imagines its prohibitions lifted – if, then, one may take any woman one pleases as a sexual object, if one may without hesitation kill one's rival for her love or anyone else who stands in one's way, if, too, one can carry off any of the other man's belongings without asking leave – how splendid, what a string of satisfactions one's life would be!

(Freud 1961b: 15)

Bertrand Russell once described his friend the novelist Joseph Conrad as a rigid moralist who 'thought of civilized and morally tolerable life as a dangerous walk on a thin crust of barely cooled lava which at any moment might break and let the unwary sink into fiery depths' (Russell 1956: 82). This vivid description equally applies to Freud. Freud's largely negative view of civilization as oppressive and provocative of neurosis prompts the deduction that his rigid obsessional control over his own impulses was a burden to him.

The same consideration goes some way to explaining why the application of psychoanalytic theory to anthropology, religion and art has been on the whole disappointing. A point of view which emphasizes the restrictions of civilization at the expense of its adaptive value is bound to be inadequate. One of the most abiding impressions which I have received from re-reading so much of Freud is that it was a pity that he cast his psychoanalytic net so widely. Freud was a wonderfully acute clinician. For example, his account of severe depression in *Mourning and Melancholia*, or his delineation of the anal character-type, are descriptions derived directly from his observation of patients which are as compelling today as when he wrote them. If psychoanalysis had remained confined within the analyst's office, it would have retained a higher status than it does today. But Freud, very early in the history of psychoanalysis, determined that it was a psychology which applied as much to the normal person as to the neurotic; and did not hesitate to explain virtually every human endeavour, from painting pictures to making jokes, in psychoanalytic terms.

Josef Breuer, Freud's first collaborator, who was originally one of his closest friends, and who supported him financially, eventually found that he could not accept Freud's theory that premature sexual experience was the cause of every case of hysteria. Freud could not tolerate this divergence from his views, and the two men became estranged. When, many years later, they encountered one another in the street, Breuer opened his arms to Freud, but Freud was so unforgiving that he ignored him and marched briskly by. Breuer was surely percipient when he wrote: 'Freud is a man given to absolute and exclusive formulations: this is a psychical need which, in my opinion, leads to excessive generalization' (Sulloway 1979: 85). This tendency is particularly evident when we consider Freud's views on the causal importance of sex in the genesis of the neuroses. As those who have read the earliest psychoanalytic papers will recall, Freud's original work with hysterical patients led him to conclude that 'Whatever case and whatever symptom we take as our point of departure, *in the end we infallibly come to the field of sexual experience*' (Freud 1962: 199). He also wrote: '*no hysterical symptom can arise from a real experience alone, but that in every case the memory of earlier experiences awakened in association to it plays a part in causing the symptom*' (Freud 1962: 197). In the same paper, Freud continues:

> I therefore put forward the thesis that at the bottom of every case of hysteria there are *one or more occurrences of premature sexual experience*, occurrences which belong to the earliest years of childhood, but which can be reproduced through the work of psycho-analysis in spite of the intervening decades. I believe this is an important finding, the discovery of a *caput Nili* in neuropathology.
>
> (Freud 1962: 203)

These statements were made on the basis of eighteen cases of hysteria; and this figure of eighteen is Freud's last attempt to give figures concerning the aetiology of any form of neurosis. Even in this instance, there were no controls; and, as we know from later examples, some of the patients concerned may have let themselves be overpersuaded by Freud's eager interpretations.

In the light of modern knowledge, it is interesting to speculate on why Freud so specifically picked on sex. He must have known that other emotions could be implicated in causing hysterical symptoms. For instance, constriction in the throat can be the consequence of being unable to 'swallow' an insult. Hysterical headaches, or even fugues, are often manoeuvres unconsciously designed to remove the sufferer from an intolerable situation, which need not be sexual in origin. The cases of so-called 'shell shock' during the First World War are good examples. Today, we seldom see the gross cases of conversion hysteria in women on which psychoanalytic theory was originally based. Did Freud never consider that social factors other than sex might be involved in aetiology? Bertha Pappenheim, Breuer's famous case, Anna O., developed gross hysterical symptoms in the fall of 1880 after nursing her seriously ill father for several months. Her father eventually died in the spring of 1881. Whatever may have been the Oedipal relation between Bertha and her father, there is no reason to suppose that sexual experiences, or even sexual phantasies, were the principal cause of her symptoms. Breuer writes that she devoted her whole energy to nursing her father until she became ill by developing a severe nervous cough. To her great sorrow, or so it appeared, she was no longer allowed to continue nursing the patient. It seems fairly obvious that, however much she adored her father, her hysterical symptoms served the purpose of removing her from duties which had become distasteful as well as unfulfilling.

Sex appealed to Freud as a root cause of neurosis because, as he told Jung in a letter, it furnished him with 'the indispensable "organic foundation" without which a medical man can only feel ill at ease in the life of the psyche' (McGuire 1979: 140–1). Sex, because it gives rise to so many psychological manifestations like dreams and phantasies, and yet is so obviously physical, bridges the gap between mind and body. Freud became more and more convinced that the chief characteristic of the neurotic person was the lack of a normal sex life, and that sexual fulfilment was the key to happiness and psychic equilibrium. Conversely, he supposed that 'if the *vita sexualis* is normal, there can be no neurosis' (Freud 1953a: 274). Although, by 1897, Freud had abandoned his *Project for a Scientific Psychology* in which he attempted to link cerebral anatomy and physiology with mental functions, he retained the hope that neurosis could ultimately be explained in physical terms.

Freud's initial belief that hysteria was caused by actual premature sexual experience was later abandoned in favour of the supposition that neurotic symptoms were related to the persistence of repressed infantile sexual phantasies which interfered with the process of sexual maturation. The reasons for this change have been so widely discussed that I shall not weary you with them. Let it suffice to quote Freud's remark: 'A formula begins to take shape which lays it down that the sexuality of neurotics has remained in, or been brought back to, an infantile state' (Freud 1953b: 172). On this basis rest Freud's theories of infantile sexual development through the various stages from oral to genital, the Oedipus complex, castration complex, penis envy and his explanations of sexual perversions.

Freud's tendency to what Breuer called absolute and exclusive formulations led him into some absurdities. For example, he made psychosexual development so central that he conceived that all other forms of social and emotional development took origin from it. In his essay on Leonardo, Freud even derives the desire for knowledge from what he called sublimated infantile sexual researches. With his Darwinian background and his fondness for dogs, Freud must have known that animals exhibit exploratory behaviour which is obviously adaptive in providing information about the environment. The exploratory drive is more closely analogous to the human desire for knowledge than is the child's sexual curiosity. Some of Freud's psychosexual assumptions have already been shown to be false: for instance, that harsh toilet training causes arrest at the anal stage, and hence predisposes to obsessional neurosis; or that there is a 'latency period' in which sexual preoccupation and play are less in evidence. It is extremely unlikely that infantile amnesia, our inability to recall the events of our first years of life, is the result of repression of our earliest sexual impulses, as Freud supposed. But, if we take Freud's theories in general rather than in particular – a manoeuvre which he would have hated – we must acknowledge a debt to him for emphasizing sexuality as a centrally important feature of the human condition, and for underlining the fact that, in the field of sex, as in other fields, the emotional climate in which the child is reared is often decisive.

Freud is justly famous for pointing out that human beings are far less masters in their own mental houses than they had previously supposed. The voice of the intellect was persistent as well as soft, but people were far more governed by emotion and irrationality than they commonly realized; and Freud affirmed that even the loftiest human achievements in the arts and philosophy were sublimations of primitive instinct. Darwin had shaken human self-esteem by demonstrating their kinship with other animals, thus dispelling the notion that man was a special creation in God's image, and reducing much human behaviour to simple biological origins. Freud was attempting to do the same thing, and one reason why psychoanalysis became so influential was that it appeared to be in line with the new biology.

Freud's tripartite division of mind into ego, superego and id was not formulated until towards the end of the First World War. But Freud's sharp distinction between the emotional and the rational, which he adumbrated as modes of mental operation called 'primary process' and 'secondary process', goes right back to the *Project for a Scientific Psychology*, which he partially abandoned in 1895, but which continued to influence his thinking.

The id is defined as 'the realm of the illogical'; 'a chaos or cauldron of seething excitations'. It is primitive and unorganized, and operates by 'primary process', governed only by a striving to satisfy instinctive needs subject to the observance of the pleasure principle. It represents the fiery depths below the level of barely cooled lava on which people like Freud and Conrad feel themselves to be dangerously poised. It is important to note that it is not assumed to display any capacity to order, sort or rearrange; it is simply untamed, chaotic desire which seeks whatever direct or indirect expression it can find.

The ego, originally defined from bodily sensations, acts as an intermediary between the id and the external world. Unlike the id, it is at any rate partly subject to the reality principle, and employs secondary process; that is, it operates by reason and common sense, and possesses the power to delay immediate responses to external stimuli or to internal instinctive promptings. In Freud's view, the way in which a scientist links concepts to make a new discovery, or by which an artist orders and shapes his or her material, is directed by the ego as a result of conscious deliberation and choice.

We have already observed that Freud regarded civilization as harshly restrictive of the 'natural man'. King Kong about to burst his bonds is the picture which springs to my mind, and which may do to yours if you have ever seen either version of the movie. It seems to me that many of the more questionable aspects of Freud's thought are derived from this dichotomy between consciousness and the unconscious, between reason and emotion, or, as E.M. Forster would have called it, between the monk and the beast.

We have seen that Freud equated 'neurotic' with 'infantile'. According to this view, neurotics were, regarding their symptoms although not in other respects, children who were still governed by the pleasure principle rather than by the reality principle: immature beings who could only fulfil their desires in phantasy rather than by moulding events in the real world. He wrote: 'We may lay it down that a happy person never phantasies, only an unsatisfied one. The motive forces of phantasies are unsatisfied wishes, and every single phantasy is the fulfilment of a wish, a correction of an unsatisfying reality' (Freud 1959: 146). Freud thought that phantasy was derived from play; and that both play and phantasy involved turning away from, or denying, reality. Such activities, therefore, ought to be outgrown. Freud took a puritanical view about how the mind should function. Life that is real is also life that is earnest. Away with play, dreams, daydreams, castles in the air! The person who is really grown up and who is not neurotic should use only conscious planning and rational thought to find satisfaction for his or her desires and should abandon the illusions of the imagination.

I do not believe that even the most hard-headed natural scientist really thinks like this. Surely every inventive person, whether operating in the arts or in the sciences, needs to 'play with concepts', as Einstein put it. Indeed, play is a vital precursor of innovation; and when artists and scientists cease to play because of overintense involvement with what they are doing, they also cease to have fruitful ideas. In the Freudian scheme, however, imagination carries a negative sign. It is always conceived as an avoidance of reality, never as being concerned with adapting to reality.

These considerations partially explain why Freud's interpretations of art and literature are unsatisfactory. Freud believed that sublimation of unsatisfied libido was responsible for all such expressions of the human spirit. Because art and literature originate from the imagination, Freud classifies them along with play, daydreams and phantasies as escapist, wish-fulfilling activities. Although Freud considered that sublimation was necessarily employed by normal people living under the constraints imposed by civilization, the implication of Freud's view must be that, if libido were fully discharged, art and literature would not be necessary.

The absurdity of this implication is evident. Freud's negative view rests upon two assumptions. The first is that phantasy, like hysterical symptoms, is necessarily derived from unsatisfied, infantile libidinous strivings, and is therefore unrealistic. The second is that the unconscious is simply chaotic and lacks any capacity for selection or order.

Some phantasies can certainly be dismissed as 'idle' daydreams. We have all had erotic and ambitious phantasies which led nowhere. But all phantasies are not like this. In trying to understand the world, in striving to come to terms with reality, we constantly employ phantasy, partly derived from memory of past experience. Anticipating a new, perhaps alarming situation, we picture to ourselves what it will be like. We imagine a variety of possibilities and how we might react to them. In other words, we use phantasy to prepare ourselves for facing reality.

Phantasy is sometimes escapist, but it is also often *adaptive*. I think that Freud's insistence that phantasy is always escapist, and that infantile sexual wishes are the roots of all phantasy and all neurosis, the 'indispensable organic foundation' of which he wrote to Jung, led him into a blind alley. It is a good example of his tendency toward overgeneralization.

Freud's assumption that the id is chaotic and lacks any capacity for selection or order might have been modified if he had examined the creative process in more detail. Graham Wallas described four stages of the creative process which he named *preparation, incubation, illumination* and *verification*. Preparation is the stage in which a problem is investigated in all directions as thoroughly as possible. This stage is consciously controlled, under the direction of the will, and closely resembles the type of mental activity which Freud named 'secondary process'.

The second stage, *incubation*, is very different. During this stage, the problem is laid aside, often for a considerable period. Both artists and scientists describe having to abandon conscious striving in favour of passivity. Brahms described the germ of musical inspiration as a 'gift' which, for a time, must be disregarded as completely as possible. He wrote:

The idea is like the seed-corn; it grows imperceptibly in secret.... I think no more of it for perhaps half a year. Nothing is lost, though. When I come back to it again it has unconsciously taken a new shape, and is ready for me to begin working at it.

(Maitland 1911: 69–70)

Similar descriptions are given by the mathematicians Poincaré and Gauss. It must be the case, therefore, that some kind of scanning, sorting or ordering process is going on unconsciously, which, eventually, may or may not create a new pattern or solve a problem. The unconscious is not merely a chaotic garbage can steaming with incestuous phantasies, but an area of mind in which, without the intervention of the will, goes on that search for order and meaning which is the common factor linking the strivings of both artists and scientists.

These considerations also apply to what Freud considered the most important of all his discoveries: the meaning of dreams. Freud believed that dreams were also escapist and infantile, and should be classified along with play and daydreams. In 1931, only eight years before his death, Freud wrote a new preface to the third English edition of *The Interpretation of Dreams* in which he said:

This book, with the new contribution to psychology which surprised the world when it was published (1900), remains essentially unaltered. It contains, even according to my present-day judgment, the most valuable of all the discoveries it has been my good fortune to make. Insight such as this falls to one's lot but once in a lifetime.

(Freud 1953c: xxxii)

In the climate of the time, it was bold of Freud to affirm that dreams, which are fleeting and unreproducible, and which depend upon subjective reports, could be treated as objects of scientific scrutiny. In 1900, the electroencephalo-gram had not been invented and the discovery of REM sleep was still fifty years away. Modern research tends to indicate that dreams are connected with some kind of scanning or sorting process in the brain, but their exact function still eludes us. Freud was surely prescient in recognizing them as important phenomena, but his explanation of them has not stood the test of time. Freud's dream theory reflects his single-mindedness, his ingenuity, and his tendency to generalization.

Freud affirmed that, with very few exceptions, dreams were disguised, hallucinatory fulfilments of repressed wishes. He also assserted, in line with his theory of hysteria, that dreams not only represented current wishes, but were also invariably expressions of wish-fulfilments dating from early childhood. He wrote: 'Our theory of dreams regards wishes originating in infancy as the indispensable motive force for the formation of dreams' (Freud 1953c: 589). Because these wishes are unacceptable and potentially disturbing, they are censored and disguised. Hence, what the dreamer recalled was only the more or less acceptable 'manifest content'. The 'latent content', consisting of unacceptable infantile sexual wishes, could only be determined when the manifest content had been subjected to psychoanalytical scrutiny and interpretation.

This theory of the meaning of dreams is notably ingenious in several ways. Freud had already decided that infantile sexual wishes were the causal agents in neurosis. We have already noted that he linked dreams, together with play and phantasy, as primitive, regressive and childish. Since both normal and neurotic persons dream, Freud's dream theory paved the way for establishing psychoanalysis as a general theory of the mind which applied to everyone. Since traces of infantile sexuality persisted to some degree in even the so-called 'normal' person, dreams might be viewed as safety valves allowing the indirect expression of forbidden wishes. Because Freud regarded unconscious mental activity as originating from the chaos of the id, and therefore as primitive, unorganized and unrelated to reality, it followed that dreams must be primarily concerned with infantile sexuality, the indispensable organic foundation of psychoanalytic theory, even if, at first sight, many dreams appeared to reflect quite other matters.

For example, Freud based his reconstruction of the origin of the 'Wolf Man's' neurosis on the interpretation of a nightmare in which the patient had been terrified by seeing six or seven white wolves sitting on the branches of a walnut tree which stood outside his bedroom window. The ingenious series of steps which led to Freud's interpretation of this dream occupies many pages. He finally concluded that what the manifest content of the dream concealed was that, between the ages of 1 and 2 years old, the patient had witnessed a primal scene of three acts of *coitus a tergo* between his parents. The Wolf Man had become very attached to Freud, and probably appeared to accept this reconstruction at the time. It must have been difficult to disagree with an analyst who took so much trouble and who was so distinguished and persuasive. However, in a later interview, he revealed:

> I never thought much of dream interpretation, you know. In my story, what was explained by dreams? Freud traces everything back to the primal scene which he derives from the dream. But that scene does not occur in the dream. When he interprets the white wolves as nightshirts or something like that, for example, linen sheets or clothes, that's somehow far-fetched, I think. That scene in the dream where the windows open and so on and the wolves are sitting there, and his interpretation, I don't know, these things are miles apart. It's terribly far-fetched.
>
> (Obholzer 1982: 35)

I think it probable that a good many of Freud's patients behaved and felt rather similarly. The famous 'Dora' certainly caved in because she was overwhelmed with interpretation. Re-reading Freud leads to the ironic conclusion that his dream theory, the 'discovery' on which he most prided himself, is one of the least convincing parts of psychoanalytic theory.

Another blind alley was Freud's excursion into anthropology, *Totem and Taboo*. Since it was first published in 1913, before modern anthropology became established, we should forgive Freud his reliance on 'armchair' theorists like Sir James Frazer, the author of *The Golden Bough*. But can we forgive so convinced a disciple of Darwin the fact that, when it suited him, he adhered to the Lamarckian belief that acquired characteristics could be inherited? Freud believed that primitive human beings lived in small groups or 'hordes', dominated by a single, powerful male, who not only kept all the females for himself, but also forcefully expelled his younger male rivals. Freud suggested that: 'One day the brothers who had been driven out came together, killed and devoured their father and so made an end of the patriarchal horde' (Freud 1958: 141). Freud thought that this primal slaughter of the father was a real event which, to use his own words, had left 'ineradicable traces in the history of humanity'. One such trace was a severe sense of guilt, which not only led to the young males renouncing claim to the women left behind by their murdered father, but also resulted in the taboo forbidding killing of the totem animal which, in Freud's view, represented the father. The totemic feast, which Freud supposed to be more common than it is, was a repetition of the criminal deed, and a reaffirmation of the taboo against sex within the totemic group. Freud called it 'man's earliest festival', 'the beginning of so many things – of social organization, of moral restrictions and of religion'. Freud pointed out that, if his interpretation of totemism is accepted, its fundamental taboos, those against incest and the slaughter of the father, corresponded with the two repressed wishes of the Oedipus complex. Freud must have felt a sense of triumph at his ingenuity. His single-mindedness and his capacity for generalization had combined to create a theory which derived the whole of morality, religion and social organization from the Oedipus complex, which he had discovered! No wonder that, to the end of his life, he refused to abandon the Lamarckian stance upon which his theory depended.

It is easy to pick holes in Freud; but I want to end by paying tribute to his legacy, and to make one or two suggestions as to why theories with so little evidence to support them swept through the Western world. First, there seems little doubt that Freud has increased our tolerance. Because of his insistence that the seeds of neurosis are sown in early childhood, we pay more attention to our children's emotional needs, and are more inclined to try to understand them rather than to punish them when they behave antisocially. Although we are still totally ineffective at dealing with criminals, there is a greater realization that savage punishments neither deter nor reform, and a greater inclination to perceive that antisocial conduct may reflect alienation from society or feelings of despair rather than innate wickedness. It used to be the case that any kind of unconventional sexual behaviour was condemned as wicked or degenerate. Because Freud insisted that men and women could be powerfully influenced by drives of which they were entirely unconscious, society is less inclined to pass facile moral judgements. We owe Freud a debt for having lifted the covers of Victorian prudery; for having emphasized the importance which the sexual drive undoubtedly plays in the lives of men and women; and for having made sex into a subject which can be openly discussed. Concurrently, psychoanalysis has made us more sceptical. Freud's reductive stance, which reduces all human striving to the lowest common denominators, has made us suspicious of those who appear morally superior. It is certainly valuable to be able to detect false pretension; the masochistic martyr who exploits the family, or the sadist who attempts moral justification of the punishments which he or she inflicts. But some believe that this deflationary tendency has gone too far; to a point at which we are so suspicious of altruism, disinterested love and self-sacrifice that we no longer acknowledge that such behaviour can be genuinely virtuous.

My personal view is that Freud's most enduring legacies are his clinical descriptions and his technique of treatment. Freud was an unrivalled clinical observer; and even if one does not agree with his causal explanations, his accounts of cases are riveting. I have already referred to his descriptions of melancholia and of the obsessional personality. We can all learn from his account of paranoia – the case of Schreber – even though we may find his interpretation of the cause of the illness in terms of repressed homosexuality quite inadequate.

If we turn to consider Freud's technique we see that every one of the innumerable varieties of subsequent forms of psychotherapy is indebted to him. The revolutionary nature of Freud's procedure and the effect which this has upon neurotic patients is still underestimated. In Freud's day, physicians were even more authoritarian than they are today; they were great men whom the patient humbly consulted, and who handed out prescriptions, instructions, advice and reassurance with a confidence derived from professional training and social prestige. Freud's abandonment of hypnosis signalled a totally different professional stance. His realization that the neuroses had mysterious origins, combined with his passion for investigation, led him to adopt a technique in which the conventional pretensions of the physician had to be dropped. He realized that, if he were to understand his patients, he must remain for most of the time a passive listener, relinquishing authority, and handing over the initiative to the patient. Free association was revolutionary, and so were its consequences. It was Freud who taught us how to listen. Free association abolished the conventional medical model of treatment in which the physician is the active agent doing something to the relatively passive patient. By compelling the patient to take the initiative, free association transformed psychoanalysis into a form of therapy in which patients, by means of interpretation and the undoing of repression, learned how best to help themselves rather than relying on prescriptions or doctor's orders. Any form of psychotherapy worth the name has adopted this as a cardinal principle.

And it was surely because of Freud's adoption of free association that he became compelled to consider his own significance in the emotional life of the patient. Our understanding of transference, which is perhaps the most important single factor in any form of analytically oriented therapy today, came about because, when Freud told his patients to associate freely, he found that they inevitably talked about their attitudes to himself. You will remember that Freud at first found this acutely distasteful and referred to the transference as a curse. His ideal was to be accepted as a skilled technician or 'mountain guide'. But his patients forced him to reconsider; and, although today we may view transference rather differently from the way in which Freud regarded it, we owe him an enormous debt for having been the first to draw attention to the phenomenon.

Perhaps Freud was lucky in being born when he was. At the time at which his main theories about the mind were being formulated, Darwin's ideas on evolution and the 'descent of man' had recently won acceptance. Darwin, by demonstrating that human beings were not a special creation, but simply the most highly evolved primates, had paved the way for a psychology which was not based upon the philosophy of mind, nor upon perception, conditioned reflexes, nor humanity's spiritual qualities, but which was rooted in human kinship with animals. The time was ripe for a psychology founded on 'instinct'; that is, upon the basic biological forces governing the behaviour of both human beings and animals. As I pointed out earlier, psychoanalysis shared with Darwinism the aim of reducing highly complex behaviour to simple biological origins.

Freud also belonged to the era in which physicists were beginning to discern the structure of matter. The electron was discovered in the 1890s. It is hardly fanciful to suggest that, at the beginning of this century, scientific understanding was equated with reducing structures to their elementary constituents. This may explain why some of the deficiencies of psychoanalytic theory were overlooked. Freud's purely reductive stance omits any consideration of synthesis, of the need to make new wholes out of apparently disparate entities, of *Gestalt* psychology, or of what Koestler later called 'bisociation'. It is because of these omissions that Freud's attempts

72 *Anthony Storr*

to explain the creative aspects of art and religion remain profoundly unsatisfactory.

If my re-reading of Freud has made me sceptical about many of his theories, it has also reinforced my conviction of his fundamental importance. Even if every theory which he put forward could be proved wrong, we should still be greatly in his debt. Perhaps the 'Wolf Man' got it right when, in an interview conducted towards the end of his long life, he said: 'Freud was a genius, there's no denying it. All those ideas that he combined in a system. . . . Even though much isn't true, it was a splendid achievement' (Obholzer 1982: 25).

REFERENCES

Freud, S. (1953a) 'My views on the part played by sexuality in the neuroses', in J. Strachey (ed.) *The Standard Edition of the Complete Psychological Works. Vol. VII*, London: Hogarth Press. (Original work published 1906.)
—— (1953b) 'Three essays on sexuality', in J. Strachey (ed.) *The Standard Edition of the Complete Psychological Works. Vol. VII*, London: Hogarth Press. (Original work published 1905.)
—— (1953c) *The Interpretation of Dreams*, in J. Strachey (ed.) *The Standard Edition of the Complete Psychological Works. Vol. IV*, London: Hogarth Press. (Original work published 1899.)
—— (1958) *Totem and Taboo*, in J. Strachey (ed.) *The Standard Edition of the Complete Psychological Works. Vol. XIII*, London: Hogarth Press. (Original work published 1913.)
—— (1959) 'Creative writers and day-dreaming', in J. Strachey (ed.) *The Standard Edition of the Complete Psychological Works. Vol. IX*, London: Hogarth Press. (Original work published 1908.)
—— (1961a) *Civilization and Its Discontents*, in J. Strachey (ed.) *The Standard Edition of the Complete Psychological Works. Vol. XXI*, London: Hogarth Press. (Original work published 1930.)
—— (1961b) *The Future of an Illusion*, in J. Strachey (ed.) *The Standard Edition of the Complete Psychological Works. Vol. XXI*, London: Hogarth Press. (Original work published 1927.)
—— (1962) 'The aetiology of hysteria', in J. Strachey (ed.) *The Standard Edition of the Complete Psychological Works. Vol. III*, London: Hogarth Press. (Original work published 1896.)
—— (1964) 'An outline of psychoanalysis', in J. Strachey (ed.) *The Standard Edition of the Complete Psychological Works. Vol. XXIII*, London: Hogarth Press. (Original work published 1940.)
McGuire, W. (ed.) (1974) *The Freud/Jung Letters*, trans. R. Manheim and R.F.C. Hull, London: Hogarth Press and Routledge.

Maitland, J.A.F. (1911) *Brahms*, London: Methuen.
Obholzer, K. (1982) *The Wolf Man Sixty Years Later*, trans. M. Shaw, London: Routledge.
Russell, B. (1956) 'Joseph Conrad', in *Portraits from Memory*, London: Allen and Unwin.
Sulloway, F.J. (1979) *Freud, Biologist of the Mind*, New York: Basic Books.

Plate 4 Konrad Lorenz (1903–89)
By permission of Mary Evans Picture Library

Plate 5 Nikolaas Tinbergen (1907–88)
By permission of Mary Evans Picture Library

4 Konrad Lorenz (1903–89) and Nikolaas Tinbergen (1907–88)

Robert A. Hinde

Konrad Lorenz, Austrian zoologist and ethologist, was born in Vienna on 7 November 1903, the son of an orthopaedic surgeon. In accordance with his father's wishes, he studied medicine at the University of Vienna, after completing two terms at Columbia University in New York. But his interests were always primarily in zoology. As a boy in Altenberg, he built aquaria and bird cages, and turned the garden with its ponds and animal enclosures into a small zoo, where he kept fish, birds, monkeys, dogs, cats and rabbits. Thus after receiving his MD in 1928, he went on to study for a PhD in comparative anatomy, which he received from the University of Vienna in 1933.

During this period of his life he established colonies of birds (such as the jackdaw and the greylag goose) and produced works which represented the first detailed outline of a biology of behaviour, including papers on the ethology of the social corvidae (1931), the species-specific behaviour patterns of birds (1932) and social aspects of the birds' world (1935). In his exploration of the nature of instinctive behaviour, he described the concepts of the innate releasing mechanism, imprinting (1935), sensitive periods during development and action-specific energy, culminating in a seminal paper in Folia Biotheoretica *in 1937. In that same year he became co-editor in chief of* Zeitschrift für Tierpsychologie *and was appointed lecturer in comparative anatomy and animal psychology at the University of Vienna. Around this time Lorenz also developed friendly contacts and collaborative work with the Dutch ethologist Nikolaas Tinbergen.*

In the years after the discovery of the spontaneity of instinctive behaviour patterns, Lorenz concerned himself increasingly with the behaviour of humans, even when animal observations provided the basis on which his conclusions were built. From 1940 to 1942 he held the chair of philosophy at the Albertus University of Königsberg, where he was also head of the department of general psychology. However, the Second World War interrupted his activities. Lorenz was an army doctor from 1942 to 1944, when he became a Russian prisoner of war. In 1948 he was released and returned to his native Austria.

From 1949–1951 he was head of the Institute of Comparative Ethology at Altenberg, and in 1950 was given a research station in Buldern, Westphalia, West Germany, by the Max Planck Society. In 1957 this moved to Seewiesen near Munich and became the Max Planck Institute for Behavioural Physiology, directed by Lorenz from 1961 to 1973. It rapidly became the focal point of a European school of ethology. Lorenz continued to study non-human species including ducks, geese, various species of cichlid fish and coral fish. In 1963 he collected much of his observational work and ideas in On Aggression, exploring the biological function of aggressive behaviour in animals and its implications for our understanding of aggressive behaviour in humans.

The pioneering contribution of Lorenz to the development of ethology, along with that of Tinbergen and Karl von Frisch, was eventually recognized by the award of the Nobel prize for physiology and medicine in 1973. In that year he also became director of the department of animal sociology at the Institute for Comparative Ethology of the Austrian Academy of Sciences at Altenberg and published Die Rückseite des Spiegels: Versuch einer Naturgeschichte menschlichen Erkenners (published in English in 1977 as Behind the Mirror: A Search for a Natural History of Human Knowledge).

There followed The Year of the Greylag Goose (1979) and in 1981 the English translation of Vergleichende Verhaltensforschung – The Foundations of Ethology, a statement and assessment of the major themes of his life's work. He died in 1989.

Nikolaas (Niko) Tinbergen, biologist and ethologist, was born in the Hague on 15 April 1907 and died in Oxford on 21 December 1988. Tinbergen received his education at Leiden University, where he carried out his early research. In 1949 he moved to Oxford, where he established an important centre for ethology. His work resulted in numerous prizes and honours including, in 1973, the award for the Nobel prize for physiology and medicine, which he shared with Konrad Lorenz and Karl von Frisch. In his empirical and theoretical contributions Tinbergen demonstrated that questions about the causation, development, function and evolution of behaviour were logically distinct, but interfertile. His work on animal behaviour was characterized primarily by an emphasis on simple experiments under field conditions. He worked especially with the three-spined stickleback and the herring gull. Of special importance are his studies of the nature of the stimuli that release 'instinctive' behaviour, of the evolution of behaviour, and of the nature of motivational systems.

In 1932–3 Tinbergen and his wife Elizabeth Amelie spent fourteen months living with Inuit in Greenland, and acquired an interest in the hunter-gatherer way of life. Although Tinbergen did not publish in anthropological journals, his papers included numerous discussions about the application of principles derived from the study of animals to human behaviour. These provided a major stimulus to the new discipline of human ethology. For instance, his work on social releasers and on the evolutionary processes involved in ritualization constituted a major contribution to the foundation of the comparative study of human expressive movements, and his work on animal motivation helps to throw light on the problem of human aggression. More importantly, ethological principles which he elaborated are now being used by his students and others to counter the 'cultural imperialism' of many anthropological interpretations. In recent years the Tinbergens applied principles derived from ethology to the study of childhood autism, and produced important evidence for a new form of treatment.

Source: Adapted from David L. Sills (ed.) (1968–79), International Encyclopaedia of the Social Sciences, New York: Free Press, Encyclopaedia Britannica and International Dictionary of Anthropologists, New York: Garland Publishing, with permission

Ethology is not a theory, and as a field of study it overlaps with many other disciplines. But the term 'ethology' is applied particularly to the work of students of behaviour, and especially animal behaviour, who share certain orienting attitudes to their research. They feel, for instance, that the description and classification of behaviour is a necessary preliminary to its analysis, that the behaviour of a species cannot be properly understood without some knowledge of the environment to which it has become adapted in evolution, and that questions about the function and evolution of behaviour are as valid and important as those about its immediate causation (Tinbergen 1963).

This last issue requires immediate emphasis, as it marks a major difference from psychologists. If you are asked 'Why does your thumb move in a different way from other fingers?' you could answer in terms of the immediate causation of thumb movement – the way in which nerves, muscles and bones relate. Or you could answer in terms of development, describing how the development of one finger rudiment took a course different from that of the others. Or you could give a functional answer – a hand with an opposable thumb makes it easier to pick things up or to climb trees. Finally, you might give an evolutionary answer, pointing out that our monkey-like ancestors had opposable thumbs. While psychologists have traditionally been interested in only the first two of these kinds of answers, ethologists treat them all as of equal status and, although logically distinct, as sometimes interfertile (e.g. Bateson 1986).

These orienting attitudes distinguished ethologists from most psychologists working in the 1930s, 1940s and 1950s: they tended to consider description unnecessary and to conduct experiments in unnatural laboratory environments for the sake of getting better control, and were interested only in the causation and development of behaviour. Nevertheless ethologists themselves differ widely in the problems they tackle, the level of analysis at which they work, the methods they use and the theoretical interpretations they adopt.

In 1973 the Nobel prize in physiology and medicine was awarded to three men, Konrad Lorenz, Niko Tinbergen and Karl von Frisch, who are generally regarded as the founders of modern ethology. Karl von Frisch was responsible for a vast amount of work on animals' perception, and is best known for his research on communication between honey bees. Although his work inspired others, and Tinbergen especially learned much from him, his contribution to ethology was otherwise overshadowed by those of Lorenz and Tinbergen.[1] In this chapter I focus on the early work of Lorenz and Tinbergen, and especially on the concepts they developed which were influential in the early days of ethology, attempting to show how their very different but complementary personalities led to the development of a set of concepts which, though subsequently superseded, provided a springboard from which ethology took off. I also compare briefly some of their later work on human behaviour.

Although Lorenz and Tinbergen are always seen as co-founders of ethology, their approaches differed. The result was divisions, usually friendly, within ethology. By an accident of history, Lorenz's influence was initially the more powerful in Germany and in the USA, where two research workers (E. Hess and G. Barlow) who had worked with Lorenz became established early on, whilst Tinbergen's was predominant in his native Holland and in the UK, to which he emigrated. I should therefore, perhaps, make it plain that I was much influenced by Tinbergen, who came to Oxford while I was a doctorate student. The reader might get a different view of ethology from Lorenz's relatively recent (1978) book, or from talking with his students and former colleagues.

Both Tinbergen and Lorenz came from families with academic values. Tinbergen's father was a grammar school teacher and a scholar of medieval Dutch, and there were teachers on both sides of the family. The family was a remarkable one, for it produced two Nobel prize winners (Niko, and his elder brother in economics), the Director of Energy in the Hague, another zoologist who died just as a potentially distinguished career was unfolding, and a sister who became, like the father, a school teacher. Lorenz's father, though of modest origins, had become a distinguished surgeon, who insisted that his sons be medically trained. However, after Konrad had qualified, his father acquiesced to his taking a PhD in comparative anatomy, and subsequently supported him for many years when he had no paid post.

Both Tinbergen and Lorenz had a passionate interest in animals, though this was expressed in very different ways. Lorenz like to keep animals, and had a menagerie of diverse species at his family home in Altenberg, Austria. He also studied the semi-tame geese that he had himself reared at Altenberg and later at Seewiesen, near Munich. He was not a field worker, but patiently observed, and sometimes identified with, semi-tame animals until he was able to formulate generalizations. Tinbergen, on the other hand, was a dedicated field naturalist. In an autobiographical article he ascribed his interest in natural history to the general interest in nature which had been growing in the Netherlands throughout the century, and he spent much of his youth exploring beaches, woods and polders around the Hague, and the sand dunes and pine forests near Hulshorst, where his family spent the summers. Although Tinbergen initiated much experimental work with captive animals, he worked on problems that he brought into the laboratory from the field, and he liked best of all to be in the field himself. Baerends puts the contrast between Niko Tinbergen and Konrad Lorenz thus: 'They shared a predilection for living with their animals – Niko preferably as a non-participating hidden observer and Konrad as an adopted alien member and protector' (Baerends 1991: 13).

This difference was reflected also in their relations with their students. Both were enthusiasts, superb and generous teachers, but, while Lorenz was revered as an authoritarian but benevolent father-figure, Tinbergen exuded a feeling of common enterprise. The difference in attitude to animals was also, perhaps, not unrelated to a difference in the way they approached their research. Lorenz was a thinker who tried to fit his observations, or rather to contrast his observations, with current biological and philosophical views. Tinbergen was much more empirical, observing and experimenting, adopting von Frisch's method of making the animal answer questions (Baerends 1991). Lorenz was always full of ideas, Tinbergen always careful in his deductions. A story illustrates the difference. In 1950 I walked with them down Jesus Lane in Cambridge while they discussed how often you had to see an animal do something before you could generalize that the behaviour was characteristic of the species. Lorenz said: 'At least five times.' Tinbergen laughed and clapped him on the shoulder and said, 'Don't be silly Konrad, you know you have said it when you have only seen the behaviour once.'

However, in spite of these differences in personality, Lorenz and Tinbergen shared attitudes towards research that were crucial for the development of ethology. On the one hand both rejected the vitalist view that the phenomenon of 'instinct' was unanalysable, and the misuse of *Gestalt* concepts to imply that analysis is unnecessary because the whole is more that the sum of its parts. On the other they rejected the focus of behaviourists on the input/output relations of the whole organism with neglect of the physiological 'machinery', and also, for reasons to be discussed later, the artificiality of many of the experiments of comparative psychologists.

Lorenz's early writings influenced the research of Tinbergen's group at Leiden before the two men first met in person in 1936. At this meeting it became apparent that their personalities were complementary. Lorenz liked talking and was always full of ideas, Tinbergen liked to listen and to subject ideas to critical verification. It was the beginning of a long friendship. The next year Tinbergen spent some time with Lorenz at Altenberg, where he initiated an experimental approach to analyse the stimuli eliciting the response of geese to aerial predators and the way in which geese retrieve eggs that had rolled out of the nest.

The two men were separated during the Second World War, much of which Tinbergen spent in a hostage camp in danger of being shot in reprisal for the activities of the Dutch underground, while Lorenz, in the German army, spent several years in a Soviet prisoner-of-war camp. Lorenz had acquired from his father a belief in the common destiny of all Germans, and they shared an admiration for many of the Nazi values. In addition Lorenz supported the view, not uncommon in the 1930s, that civilized man was genetically degenerate, and saw eugenic principles as offering a long-term solution. Thus some of his writing in the early war years expressed views unacceptable to Tinbergen (and many others). This nearly led to a rift, but Lorenz subsequently recanted and apologized, Tinbergen forgave and almost forgot, and the issue faded into the background behind their passionate interest in the behaviour of animals. Lorenz's (1978) retrospective account of ethology was dedicated to Niko Tinbergen.

In the mid-1930s Lorenz (1932, 1935, 1950a) was responsible for two concepts which were to have a crucial influence on the development of ethology. Observing that much species-characteristic behaviour was elicited by highly specific stimulus situations, he postulated an innate releasing mechanism (IRM) which fitted the stimulus as a lock fits a key. And noting that many movement patterns were as characteristic of a species as their anatomical features, he coined the term 'fixed action pattern' (FAP). Performance of these stereotyped FAPs usually resulted in a lowering of motivation, and they were often referred to as 'consummatory acts' to distinguish them from the more variable earlier phases of a behaviour sequence, which was said to involve 'appetitive behaviour'. These two concepts became the main planks of a comprehensive theory of instinctive behaviour which, though later modified in nearly every particular, avoided the ultimate sterility of the subjectivism then prevalent in Europe and the behaviourism which was beginning to flower in the USA.

Lorenz observed that many FAPs sometimes appeared 'spontaneously', in the absence of the normally appropriate stimulus. For example, he referred frequently to an observation of a caged starling going through the motions of catching a non-existent fly. Such action sequences which appeared in the absence of the appropriate stimulus were termed 'vacuum activities'. Lorenz therefore postulated that each FAP had its own autonomous source of motivation, which did not overlap with that of other movement patterns. He pictured this as a reservoir, filled with 'reaction specific energy', which could be discharged in behaviour either by the action of an external stimulus acting through the IRM, or by the hydrostatic pressure of the fluid in the system (Figure 4.1). In this way he could account for the fact that species-characteristic movements could be elicited either by a key stimulus or, in what seemed the absence

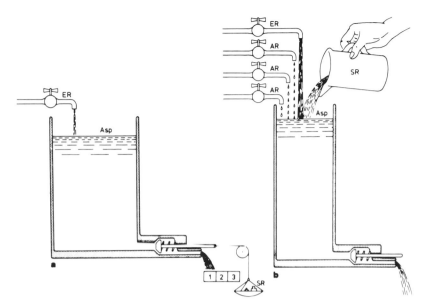

Figure 4.1 Lorenz's 'psycho-hydraulic' model of motivation
Source: Lorenz 1978 by permission of Springer-Verlag
Note: In the original version (left) the tap ER represents an endogenous source of 'action specific potential' (Asp). This can be released through the spring valve either by the action of an external stimulus, pictured as weights on a scale pan (SR), or by the hydrostatic pressure overcoming the valve. The diagram on the right is a later version which minimizes the distinction between the releasing and motivating effects of stimuli and allows for a minor contribution from non-specific sources of motivation (AR).

of a stimulus, apparently by the build-up of motivation. This model, of course, had much in common with those used by Freud (1966) and McDougall (1923). Lorenz (1950a) was explicit in saying that this was an 'as if' model, and was not proposing that such reservoirs actually existed in the brain.

Experiments with sticklebacks carried out by Tinbergen and his co-workers (primarily van Iersel and Sevenster) did not confirm Lorenz's view that the several motor patterns of a species were motivationally independent. Particular stimulus situations could lower the threshold of stimulation necessary for the release of several functionally related FAPs. Since the threshold change persisted after the stimulus situation had gone, Tinbergen deduced that there had been a change in the central state relevant to several FAPs. He therefore elaborated a model of a hierarchy of

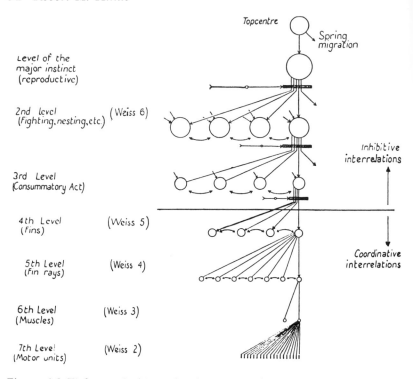

Figure 4.2 Tinbergen's hierarchical system of 'centres' underlying the 'reproductive instinct' of the three-spined stickleback
Source: Tinbergen 1951, by permission of the Oxford University Press
Note: The centres (represented by circles) immediately above the horizontal line coordinate FAPs. The higher centres motivate groups of FAPs, those below the line the several levels of effectors. Below each centre is a block which can be removed by appropriate stimuli.

centres which could be loaded with 'motivational impulses' (Figure 4.2). These were prevented from discharging until the releasing factors activated a reflex-like mechanism, the IRM, thereby removing the block. As the IRMs at successive levels were activated, the motivational impulses could load lower centres until they were eventually discharged in the performance of an FAP or consummatory act (Tinbergen 1942, 1951).

In one sense the scheme was less sophisticated than Lorenz's 'as if' hydraulic model, because it implied a close correspondence between the 'centres' and localized nervous mechanisms, and between 'motivational impulses' and nerve impulses. Indeed, Tinbergen used Hess and Brügger's (1943) demonstration that localized stimulation of the hypothalamus could elicit complete behaviour patterns to support his scheme, and drew the idea of hierarchy in part from Weiss's (1941) work on the nervous control of limb movements.

In any case, it became apparent that the concept of a unitary drive for each behaviour pattern was too simple: each pattern of behaviour was affected by many factors, some of which were general and some specific in their effects. And the 'energy' model of motivation was seen to be both misleading and incompatible with some of the data (Hinde 1956, 1960). In fact work from Tinbergen's own students contributed to the rejection of the idea that the lowering of motivation could be likened to the discharge of either 'reaction specific energy' or 'motivational impulses'. Bastock et al. (1953) showed that certain aspects of the incubation behaviour of gulls came to an end when the bird received specific stimuli ('consummatory stimuli') through its brood patch. (This concept of consummatory stimuli or a consummatory state was implicit in some of Lorenz's early writing [1937, 1966a], but he never exploited its significance.) Also important here was the earlier work of von Holst and Mittelstaedt (1950) showing how behaviour could be controlled by the difference between the stimuli impinging on the animal and 'goal' stimuli. They had suggested that an 'efference copy' in a motor centre was potentially nullified by 'reafference' returning from the effectors and exteroceptors as a result of the movement, and that movement ceased when the two coincided – in other words, when the current situation became identical with the goal. Such data indicated that a fall in motivation could not be pictured in terms of 'discharge', and thus served as powerful criticisms of both Lorenz's energy model and Tinbergen's hierarchy of centres. Tinbergen accepted the criticisms and modified his views. Lorenz (1978) acknowledged them but produced an amended version which embraced more facts but evaded the basic issues.

However, Tinbergen's hierarchy did embrace another issue which has come to have central importance in ethology. Rejecting the Lorenzian view of the independence of motor patterns, Tinbergen's hierarchy emphasized the

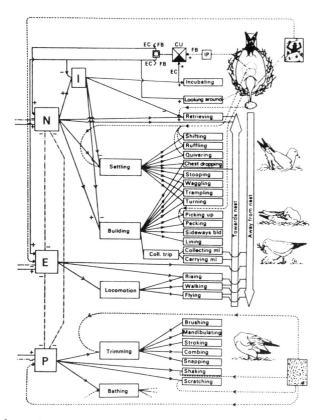

Key to main elements:
I – inhibitory system (operating when feedback matches expectancy)
N – incubation system
E – escape system
P – preening system

Figure 4.3 Three behaviour systems postulated to describe the occurrence of interruptive behaviour during the incubation of the herring gull
Source: Baerends and Drent 1970: 267, by permission of E.J. Brill, Leiden
Note: FAPs are shown to the right, first- and second-order control systems to the left. The large arrows represent orientation with respect to the nest, the thin arrows the relations between the systems.

relations between them. This reflected the earlier work of Baerends (1941; Baerends and Baerends-van Roon 1950), Tinbergen's first student, on the relations between different patterns of behaviour shown by hunting wasps and cichlid fishes, and led to the concept of the 'behaviour system' – a 'black box' model of the causal relations between different functionally related activities (Baerends 1976) (Figure 4.3). In a qualitative way this concept has had a considerable impact not only in ethology but also in the field of child development, in accounting for the relationship between mother and child. Bowlby (1969) postulated an 'attachment behaviour system' in the child, interaction between it and other systems (fear, exploration) and the 'parenting behaviour system' accounting for many of the variations in the parent–child relationship.

Lorenz's concept of the FAP had another important influence on Tinbergen's research. Lorenz (1941), following the earlier work of Heinroth (1911), used comparisons between the several display movements of ducks, geese and swans to trace the phylogenetic relations between species. Tinbergen acquired from Lorenz a realization of the power of the comparative method (Tinbergen 1952). Its use for tracing the course of evolution raised the complementary question of how the often bizarre display movements themselves had evolved. Tinbergen saw that displays or the elements of displays could be seen as directly descended from other activities functional in a different way. For instance, many threat movements contain elements of locomotory movements. This led to two further lines of work. First, the course of the evolution of display movements could be traced by comparative studies: the processes by which they became more effective for a signal function were collectively termed 'ritualization' – elaboration of the movement, the development of conspicuous structures which rendered them more effective, and so on (Tinbergen 1948, 1952).

Second, many displays could be seen as composed of elements of incompatible types of behaviour – attack and escape, or approach and withdrawal, for example. This led to the view that the initially incomprehensible display

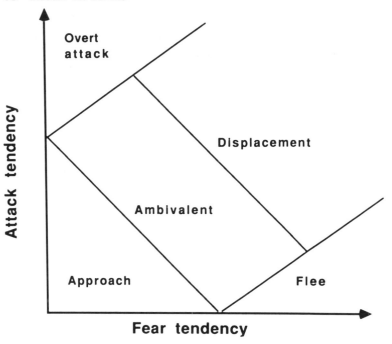

Figure 4.4 Graphical representation of Tinbergen's conflict theory of agonistic behaviour
Source: Huntingford 1991, by permission of Chapman & Hall
Note: It is supposed that the behaviour shown depends on the absolute and relative levels of tendencies to attack and flee from the rival

movements used in fighting and courtship resulted from the simultaneous arousal of incompatible tendencies. The essence of the idea is shown in Figure 4.4. In an agonistic situation, the primary tendencies involved would be to attack and to flee. If one of these were much stronger than the other, the animal would attack or flee. When they were at least moderately strong and in balance, it would either show ambivalent behaviour, such as a threat posture, or an apparently irrelevant 'displacement' activity. This hypothesis brought order into the whole field of the comparative study of signal movements (Huntingford 1991). However, Tinbergen had supposed that the several display movements of a species carried a true message of the strengths and relative strengths of the behavioural tendencies involved, and thus predicted what it would do next.

It has more recently been argued that this would be mal-adaptive: in a fight, it is best to conceal your intentions (Maynard Smith 1979). Dawkins and Krebs (1978; Krebs and Dawkins 1984) therefore suggested that signals made in non-cooperative situations would result in an 'arms race' of per-suasion by the actor and resistance by the reactor, leading to conspicuous, ritualized signals, with the participants manipulating each other, while in cooperative situations, where it is in the reactors' interests to respond, the actors will not have evolved conspicuous signals because the actors do not need to be coerced to respond. Whilst these authors emphasized manipulation, Zahavi (e.g. 1975) has emphasized that signals must indicate honestly something in the actor which is important to the reactor, such as health or fighting ability. Thus having a large red comb on one's head, or carrying heavy antlers, could indicate that the individual was sufficiently well endowed to succeed in spite of the self-imposed handicap – just as humans use unnecessarily expensive artefacts to demonstrate their power (Rawson 1992). Discussion of how these approaches can be reconciled (Krebs 1991) and of the impact of games theory on the study of signals (Maynard Smith and Parker 1976) would take us beyond our present brief.

Lorenz's concept of the IRM also had an important impact on Tinbergen's research. Lorenz had based it on observa-tion and intuition; Tinbergen subjected it to experimental verification. Studies, now classics of ethology, demon-strated the role of the red belly of the male three-spined stickleback in eliciting agonistic behaviour, and of the red spot on a herring gull's bill in eliciting begging from a chick (e.g. Tinbergen and Perdeck 1950). However, it is also clear that the emphasis on the release of responses by a few key stimuli was overdone: responsiveness is always multiply determined (Huntingford 1991).

It will be apparent that the two concepts of FAP and IRM played a crucial role in the early development of ethology. Fascinating from the history-of-science point of view is the fact that subsequently each of them came to be seen as flawed in many respects. Fixed action patterns turned out

90 *Robert A. Hinde*

not to be so fixed as had earlier been thought, but somewhat variable (Barlow 1977). As we have seen, they are not independently motivated, but may share motivational factors. And the hydraulic model associated with them turned out to be unacceptable. Nevertheless, the core idea of adaptive differences in behaviour (FAPs, but also responsiveness and predispositions to learn: see below) remains of central importance. And the innate releasing mechanism turned out not to be innate (as the key stimuli could be modified by experience), not to be solely releasing (as the distinction between the releasing and motivating effects of stimuli implied by Tinbergen's hierarchical model proved to be invalid, while stimuli also can have inhibiting and orienting functions), and not a single mechanism, but a complex of mechanisms with properties that vary according to the state of the animal. Yet there remain the facts of selective perception, the finding that some responses are elicited by simple, highly specific stimulus situations, and the observation that in many cases the relations between stimulus and response are independent of previous experience of the stimulus. It is as though the concepts of FAP and IRM each referred to important principles but, in the growing pains of a developing science, were reified too soon.

Although Lorenz and Tinbergen are primarily associated with the study of 'instinct', each of them was also concerned with the modification of behaviour. Tinbergen's contribution here was modest but, for instance, many of his early experiments were concerned with the way in which digger wasps learned the location of their nests so that they could relocate them after a foraging trip (Tinbergen 1932 and 1935; see also Baerends 1941). Lorenz's belief in the unmodifiability of instinctive patterns led him to insist that learning was somehow 'intercalated' between more rigid elements. This has not proved fruitful. However, his focus on 'imprinting' has had important consequences. 'Imprinting' is the process by which young ducks and geese will learn to follow a wide range of moving objects, showing behaviour that would naturally be directed to their parents, and which may affect late social and sexual preferences. Lorenz (e.g.

1935) claimed that imprinting was a form of learning, special in that (1) it is confined to a brief period of the life-cycle, (2) it is irreversible, in the sense that once a bird has learned to follow one object it will not follow others, (3) it may be completed long before the responses to which it will later refer have developed, (4) it involves learning of species rather than individual characteristics, and (5) it does not depend on any conventional reward. Some of these characteristics now seem to be invalid. For instance, the period during which learning can occur is more flexible than Lorenz supposed and can be influenced by external factors; the learning is not necessarily irreversible; and the learning of individual characteristics takes place along with that of specics characteristics (Hinde 1962). Nevertheless, the broad concept of imprinting is still a valuable one. Although the relation of imprinting to other forms of learning is still not clear (Bateson 1990), it has provided us with an extremely valuable model for the study of the neural mechanisms underlying learning in vertebrates (Horn 1985), and it influenced the early development of attachment theory (Bowlby 1969; see Rutter 1992 for critique).

As we have seen, Lorenz influenced Tinbergen to use the comparative method to study the evolution of behaviour. This work was carried forward in a remarkable way by his students (e.g. Moynihan 1959). Tinbergen himself also initiated work on the function of behaviour, mostly with field experiments. For example, he asked 'Why do black-headed gulls remove the eggshells from the nest after the young hatch, when doing so leaves the nest briefly unprotected?' Noting that the outside of the eggshell is camouflaged while the inside is conspicuously white, he was able to show experimentally that the proximity of a broken eggshell increased the susceptibility of the remaining eggs to predation (Tinbergen *et al*. 1962).

Another difference between the two founders of ethology is worth noting here. In the early days, theorists writing about evolution did not distinguish between natural selection acting on the individuals and the possible effects of natural selection between groups of individuals. In the

1960s it came to be generally recognized that intergroup selection was unlikely to be important, and that natural selection acted mainly if not entirely on the differences between individuals. This was mostly accepted by Tinbergen, but Lorenz continued often to write in group selection terms.

The achievement of Lorenz and Tinbergen in establishing ethology cannot be understood fully if it is assumed that its development took place in a vacuum. There was the background of subjective psychology on the one hand and behaviourism on the other: both Lorenz and Tinbergen felt that these were giants to be toppled. But certain individuals played crucial roles as friends or foes. In 1935 F.A. Beach had independently developed in the USA methods of using models to analyse the stimuli controlling behaviour. When Tinbergen met Beach in 1938 the two men had a common language. Tinbergen's comments are revealing:

> Although at that time I was not at all attracted to Frank's 'lab-orientedness', nor to his inclination to measure simple components of the 'causal web', he on his side was open-minded enough (I am sure not merely polite enough) to express interest in what we were then doing. And he did influence us, much to the good, by his insistence on the need for measurement. I think that it was a combination of our respect for his research, for his open-mindedness and for his friendly and truly cooperative attitude that made us approach him for representing *Behaviour* in the US.
>
> (Tinbergen, personal communication)

(The 'us' includes W.H. Thorpe, the British entomologist and ethologist who subsequently did much to publicize and advance ethological ideas. He started the Madingley laboratory where I have been fortunate to work since 1950.) 'Beach has never called himself an ethologist, perhaps because he viewed the early ethologists' "field-orientedness" as "fine, but not for me"', but he continued to be both a fellow traveller and a friendly critic' (Tinbergen, personal communication).

However, other comparative psychologists, led by T.C. Schneirla, were strongly opposed to the new discipline. There were a number of issues. First, Schneirla was bitterly opposed to Lorenz's distinctions between innate and acquired behaviour, arguing that it was neither empirically useful nor heuristically valuable, and that it led to a neglect of the complex processes occurring in development. In his view, bringing up animals in social isolation was not adequate evidence that the behaviour that appeared was innate, but merely showed that it was independent of some of the external factors that might have been thought to be important. Second, Schneirla was strongly opposed to 'energy models' of motivation, such as Lorenz's hydraulic model described above. Third, he stressed the importance of recognizing the differences between levels in the cognitive capacities of animals. He was therefore wary of terms like 'aggressive behaviour' which involved very different mechanisms in ant, goose and human being.

On their side, the ethologists had their own reservations about psychology, though they did not always distinguish too clearly between its varieties, and some of their criticisms were based on ignorance. For instance, Lorenz (1958), better acquainted with European than American 'comparative' psychology, simply regarded psychology as a science dealing with subjective phenomena. But the ethologists despised the way in which American psychologists based far-reaching generalizations on data from very few mammalian species (mostly the laboratory rat), and felt that the adjective 'comparative' was a sham, for contrasting distantly related species of different phyletic levels did not constitute comparison in a biological sense.

Schneirla's criticisms tended to be written with a difficult prose style and published in journals not widely read by ethologists. However, in 1953 his pupil, Daniel Lehrman, published 'A critique of Konrad Lorenz's theory of instinctive behaviour' in the *Quarterly Review of Biology*. Although toned down on the advice of Frank Beach, Ernst Mayr and others, this was a hard-hitting attack on ethology. Surprisingly, it led to a permanent rapprochement between most ethologists and, with the exception of a few comparative psychologists who remained hostile partly on political grounds, most comparative psychologists. This was almost entirely due to personal factors. Lorenz has described how, after reading the critique, he pictured Lehrman as a pinched, shrivelled little man. Nothing could be further from the truth. Lehrman weighed much more than he should have, had an infectious personality, and an ebullience and enthusiasm for natural history comparable to Lorenz's. Like Lorenz and Tinbergen, he was a bird watcher, and both took to him as soon as they met him.

As a result, both sides changed their emphasis. Comparative psychologists withdrew from their extreme emphasis on the role of experience, and ethologists came to realize that the distinction between learned and innate behaviour was invalid, though that between genetic and environmental sources of difference was valuable and led to constructive advance (e.g. Bateson 1987; Hinde 1968, 1983; Oyama 1985). Tinbergen came to accept this position fully. Lorenz (e.g. 1961) changed his ground somewhat, arguing that the concept of innateness should be related to the adaptedness of behaviour rather than to its development. On this view, the *fit* between the behaviour of a species and its environment could be due either to genetic programming or to experience. More importantly, he went on to emphasize that there are species differences in what animals learn, so there must be species-characteristic ('innate') predispositions to learn some things rather than others. Thus Baerends (1941) had emphasized the amazing ability of the wasp *Ammophila campestris* to modify its foraging behaviour as a consequence of 'inspection visits' made to the holes where its larvae were developing, although its learning capacity in other contexts was meagre. This emphasis on predispositions to learn has borne fruit. For instance, Thorpe (1961) showed that male chaffinches have to learn their song, but can only learn songs with a note structure similar to that of normal chaffinch song (see also Seligman and Hager 1972; Hinde and Stevenson-Hinde 1973).

Furthermore, as discussed above, most ethologists abandoned energy models of motivation. On the 'comparative' issue, the differences in approach were recognized. The problem of accounting for the diverse levels of complexity within the animal kingdom, and the problem of micro-evolution within animal groups with which the ethologists were concerned, were both seen as important. In due course, comparative psychologists came to see the value of studying a wide range of species and of taking account of the animals' natural environment.

Thus at one time at least some ethologists and some comparative psychologists saw themselves as bitterly opposed to each other. Lehrman's 'Critique' established a dialogue which, largely because of the personalities of the participants, was constructive and led in the main to a permanent rapprochement between most members of both groups. On the whole the relations of comparative psychologists to Tinbergen and others influenced by him was closer than that to Lorenz and his colleagues. Some debate between Lehrman (e.g. 1970) and Lorenz continued (see Beer 1975), but Lehrman effectively joined the ethologists. Whilst at the present time some comparative psychologists influenced by Schneirla still reject ethology and there are a few ethologists who perpetuate the notion of innate behaviour, on the whole the distinction between the two groups barely exists. This came about not through one group proving the other wrong, though this happened over some issues, but by a combination of tenacity by members of each side where they continued to believe themselves right with humility and a willingness to learn.

As I have tried to point out, these two scientists, whose interactions were to have such a profound effect on behavioural science, had very different personalities. Nowhere is this displayed more clearly than in their writings about their own species.

Lorenz's writings about human behaviour started in the 1930s. Much of what he wrote was anecdotal and second-hand, and his pontifical style, laced with phrases like 'Quite definitely' and 'It is objectively convincing, indeed it is proof', casts doubts on his occasional disclaimers that his views were 'purely hypothetical'. Nevertheless, there is much to ponder on. As a biologist, Lorenz was interested primarily in adaptation: he pointed out that our thought processes, which must have evolved in adaptation to the world about us, cannot be expected to convey absolute truths, but only a working knowledge. Thus our concepts should not be seen as true representations of an outer world, but as constructs corresponding sufficiently well with the outside world to enable individuals to behave adaptively. (Interestingly, for a while Lorenz held Kant's chair in Königsberg.) Again, as a biologist he attempted to apply some of the concepts he had found useful in studying animal behaviour to humans. He discussed at some length the presence of 'innate releasing mechanisms', focusing especially on the characteristics of small children which elicit parental behaviour (Lorenz 1950b). Subsequent research has confirmed a number of his suggestions here (Gardner and Wallach 1965; Sternglanz *et al.* 1977; Fullard and Reiling 1976). However, he linked not implausible suggestions about responses to stimulus characters to speculations about emotional responses to conventional situations in literature and films. He then came to refer to 'innate releasing mechanisms ... of an aesthetic nature – as relatively entity-independent components and skeletal elements of human social behaviour' (Lorenz 1950b: 161).

Humans have relatively few stereotyped movement patterns. Since Lorenz's concept of 'instinct' was based on that of FAPs, he therefore found less evidence for human 'instincts' in movement patterns than in responsiveness. Believing that each motor pattern was linked to a specific emotion, he had to suppose that humans have fewer 'specific feelings and passions' than animals (Lorenz 1935, 1937). Lorenz (1950b) linked these issues to the supposed domestication of human beings, which in his view involved a loss in the specificity of innate releasing mechanisms and an increased variability in the 'endogenous generation of motor impulses' whereby the more primitive 'instincts' hypertrophy (hence human hypersexuality: Lorenz 1935) and the more finely differentiated (e.g. parental behaviour) tend to disappear (1950b).

Lorenz's views about the endogenous generation of motor impulses influenced his views on the nature of human behaviour in many ways, and most especially his views on aggression, which he held to be 'instinctive'. He noted that humans lack the aggression-inhibiting gestures found in many species (1966a). He also argued it would be no use to shield individuals from aggression-eliciting stimuli, since the motivation would invariably build up and in the end burst forth in a 'vacuum activity' even in the absence of appropriate stimuli. Nor, for a similar reason, is it any use to put a moral veto on aggression (1966a). Although Lorenz emphasized the genetic bases of differences in aggression, in 1966 he argued against any attempt to weed out the aggressive drive by eugenic planning, though his reasons for this are curious. Intraspecific aggression is, he believed, intrinsic to the human reaction of enthusiasm, and this is indispensable for the achievement of the highest human goals. Furthermore, because species that do not have personal bonds also lack intraspecies aggression, Lorenz argued that aggression in very many animals and probably in human beings is an essential component of personal friendship. And, he supposed, because of the complexity of interaction between different 'drives', we do not know what would happen if one of them were to disappear. Lorenz in fact believed that many important human activities were partially motivated by aggression. 'With the the elimination of aggression . . . the tackling of a task or problem, the self-respect without which everything that a man does from morning until evening, from the morning shave to the sublimest artistic or scientific creations, would lose all impetus' (Lorenz 1966a).

Instead, Lorenz recommended catharsis – the discharge of aggressive motivation in other ways. He mentioned sport as an outlet for individual aggression and competitive sport as a substitute for international war. He suggested the arousal of enthusiasm for high-value causes other than war, the promotion of individual friendships across national boundaries, and steps to devalue warlike virtues. Art could be used to create supranational, suprapolitical values; militant enthusiasm could be directed into science; laughter and humour were to be encouraged, and so on. (Of course, seeing aggression as deeply ingrained in human nature, with 'warrior virtues' selected for in evolution, Lorenz saw the task as a hard one.)

In so far as Lorenz's cures for aggression are almost entirely based on his assumption of the endogenous generation of motivational impulses, there is no need to evaluate them here. But it is worth saying that there is evidence that external stimuli can enhance aggressive motivation (Berkowitz 1989); societal differences in the degree of violence displayed are correlated with the power of moral vetoes on violence (Whiting and Whiting 1975); the belief that aggression forms part of many laudable human activities is unproven and seems to depend on a confusion between aggressiveness and assertiveness – a confusion also inherent in such phrases as 'aggressive salesmanship'; and recent events on many football grounds serve to demonstrate that sport is not a useful way of diminishing aggressiveness (see also Berkowitz 1963). And while genetic differences may play some part in individual differences in aggression, socialization practices are far more important in instilling 'warrior virtues' (Groebel and Hinde 1989).

Although he sought for human parallels to the concepts he had found useful in animals, of course Lorenz realized the differences, laying emphasis on differences in perceptual ability (Lorenz 1935), thought processes (1954) and especially language (1935, 1966a, 1966b). He emphasized the importance of conceptual thought and tradition as together making possible rapid cultural evolution (1970, 1978). His views on the relations between individuals and society are more interesting, and in some ways before his time. He was aware of the two-way causal relations between individual and society – though he saw these as going primarily from individual to 'society' in animals, and in the opposite direction in humans: 'When young people are growing up, they are extensively moulded by the society in which they develop. When young jackdaws grow up, they form a jackdaw society complete to the last detail with no prior image' (Lorenz 1935: 255). He also believed that values, cultures, beliefs, etc., were interrelated and thus form a structure (Lorenz 1966a), an issue neglected by many social scientists today. In his later years he constantly emphasized the misfit between individuals and the demands of Western society.

Lorenz's views of human behaviour have given rise to a primarily Austrian group studying 'evolutionary epistemology' (Wuketits 1990), and we must await the results of this enterprise. It will be apparent, however, that Lorenz's discussions consist largely of extrapolations from his views on animal behaviour, with a strong admixture of folk psychology (e.g. his views on the generation gap: Lorenz 1970). Later his imitators, such as Ardrey (1967) and Morris (1967), carried the speculations even further.

Tinbergen's approach was very different. In his application of the ethological orientation to human behaviour, Tinbergen also pressed a biological viewpoint, but with considerable humility. In his earlier work the references to humans were few, and mostly involved parallels at the reflex or IRM level. Later, he argued strongly against the uncritical application of ethological results to human beings. He gave three main reasons for this. First, he thought that some authors, such as Lorenz and Morris (e.g. Morris 1967), 'present as knowledge a set of statements which are after all no more than likely guesses' (Tinbergen 1968: 1411). Second, he emphasized the ease with which examples could be plucked from the diversity of animal behaviour to suit any thesis. And third, he argued that since both our behaviour and our environment have changed so much since cultural evolution gathered momentum, it is more profitable to apply a biological approach than to look for parallels (Tinbergen 1968).

In the early 1970s, Tinbergen's pupil Blurton Jones (1972) pioneered the application of ethological methods to human behaviour. This work is remembered principally for the use of 'physical description' for children's behaviour (i.e.

description in principle capable of reduction to movements of muscles, bones, etc.). In my view this was a mistake, the greater relevance of 'description by consequence', which emphasizes the goal-directedness of much behaviour, being neglected. Children are not fish, and methods used to describe fish behaviour are not necessarily applicable to them. However, Blurton Jones also provided a masterly summary of a rather extreme ethological position, emphasizing the importance of description and the dangers of global concepts like aggression, anxiety and attachment.

Tinbergen himself also laid emphasis on the importance of description: 'Intense, long, repeated "plain" or "simple" observation, guided by a truly inquiring, not prematurely prejudiced state of mind' was the Tinbergens' (1983: 19) prescription for studying autism. He also emphasized the great importance of distinguishing the four whys, and his article 'On war and peace in animals and man' (1968) provides a brilliant overview of the manner in which each of the whys throws light on a particular problem.

In writing about aggression, Tinbergen (1968) discussed the individual factors operating and then, unlike many other writers at the time, went on to discuss the additional factors that operated in groups. He acknowledged the role of leaders and of external threats, but paid little attention to other factors (e.g. Tajfel 1978; Rabbie 1991) that enhance group formation. Unlike many other biologists, he did not underestimate the role of cultural factors in human warfare.

Tinbergen also drew lessons from ethology about education. Impressed by the learning opportunities provided by play-like activities in animals, he questioned the predominance of formal instruction over self-initiated exploration in our educational system. He stressed the need for the child to be given security in order to maximize exploration, and the need for adults to be sensitively supportive without being interfering (Tinbergen and Tinbergen 1983).

During the latter years of their lives Niko Tinbergen and his wife put most of their energies into studying childhood autism. They were convinced that the distinction between normal and autistic children was far from sharp, and that a conflict between hyperanxiety and sociality, comparable *in principle* to the conflicts Niko Tinbergen had studied in sticklebacks and gulls, was involved. They suggested that when the conflict becomes severe, the child withdraws and future socialization is severely hampered. The child then fails to learn from social interaction and exploration. Their espousal of a behavioural approach to autism brought the Tinbergens into head-on collision with many psychiatrists, who believe that autism has genetic factors and that these have a determining role. That debate continues.

Tinbergen was one of the first to become concerned about the pace of cultural change, people's influence on their environment, the depletion of non-renewable resources and the accumulation of toxic wastes. In his Croonian Lecture to the Royal Society he argued that appeals to altruism or moral arguments would be in vain – we must point out that the matter of building a new society is one of enlightened self-interest.

In conclusion, I would emphasize four points. First, there is the magnitude of the achievement of these two men. What they set in motion has had a tremendous impact on the behavioural sciences, which extends far beyond 'ethology'. Second, it is likely that this could not have been achieved by either alone, and the differences of style and personality between them were crucial. Third, and this is no reflection on the founders of ethology, virtually all the concepts on which the ethology of the 1940s and 1950s was based have turned out to be imprecise or fatally flawed; nevertheless, they led to important questions being asked. And fourth, many of the advances made in the 1950s and later stemmed from academic disputes between differing views conducted with humility and integrity.

NOTES

This article is reprinted from the *International Dictionary of Anthropologists* (New York: Galland Publishing, Inc.) 1991, by permission of the publisher.

1 For further information the reader is advised to turn to:

Dawkins, M.S., Halliday, T.R. and Dawkins, R. (eds) (1991) *The Tinbergen Legacy*, London: Chapman and Hall.
Hinde, R.A. (1990) 'Nikolaas Tinbergen', *Biographical Memoirs of Fellows of the Royal Society* 36: 549–65.
Krebs, J.R. and Sjölander, S. (1992) 'Konrad Z. Lorenz', *Biographical Memoirs of Fellows of the Royal Society* 38: 209–28.
Nisbett, A. (1976) *Konrad Lorenz*, London: Dent.
Schleidt, W.M. (ed.) (1988) *Der Kreis um Konrad Lorenz: Ideen, Hypothesen, Ansichten*, Berlin: Paul Pavey.

Autobiographical chapters are to be found in D.A. Dewsbury (ed.) (1985), *Studying Animal Behaviour: Autobiographies of the Founders*, Chicago: University of Chicago Press.

REFERENCES

Ardrey, R. (1967) *The Territorial Imperative*, New York: Atheneum.
Baerends, G.P. (1941) 'Fortpflanzungsverhalten und Orientierung der Grabwespe' *Ammophila campestris Jur. Tidschrift für Entomologie* 84: 68–275.
—— (1976) 'The functional organisation of behaviour', *Animal Behaviour* 24: 726–38.
—— (1991) 'Early ethology: growing from Dutch roots', in M.S. Dawkins, T.R. Halliday and R. Dawkins (eds) *The Tinbergen Legacy*, London: Chapman and Hall.
Baerends, G.P. and Baerends-van Roon, H.M. (1950) 'An introduction to the study of cichlid fishes', *Behaviour Supplement* 1: 1–242.
Baerends, G.P. and Drent, R.H. (1970) 'The herring gull and its egg', *Behaviour Supplement* 17.
Barlow, G.W. (1977) 'Modal action patterns', in T.A. Sebeok (ed.) *How Animals Communicate*, Bloomington, Ind.: Indiana University Press.
Bastock, M., Morris, D. and Moynihan, M. (1953) 'Some comments on conflict and thwarting in animals', *Behaviour* 6: 66–84.
Bateson, P. (1986) 'Functional approaches to behavioural development', in J.G. Else and P.C. Lee (eds) *Primate Ontogeny, Cognition and Social Behaviour*, Cambridge: Cambridge University Press.
—— (1987) 'Biological approaches to the study of behavioural development', *International Journal of Behavioural Development* 10: 1–22.
—— (1990) 'Is imprinting such a special case?', *Philosophical Transactions of the Royal Society B* 329: 125–31.
Beer, C.G. (1975) 'Was Professor Lehrman an ethologist?', *Animal Behaviour* 23: 957–64.

Berkowitz, L. (1963) *Aggression*, New York: McGraw-Hill.
—— (1989) 'Situational influences on aggression', in J. Groebel and R.A. Hinde (eds) *Aggression and War*, Cambridge: Cambridge University Press.
Blurton Jones, N. (ed.) (1972) *Ethological Studies of Child Behaviour*, Cambridge: Cambridge University Press.
Bowlby, J. (1969) *Attachment and Loss. Vol. I: Attachment*, London: Hogarth Press.
Dawkins, R. and Krebs, J.R. (1978) 'Animal signals: information or manipulation?', in J.R. Krebs and N. Davies (eds) *Behavioural Ecology*, Oxford: Blackwell.
Freud, S. (1966) 'Instincts and their vicissitudes', in J. Strachey (ed.) *The Standard Edition of the Complete Psychological Works. Vol. 14*, London: Hogarth Press. (Original work published 1915.)
Fullard, W. and Reiling, A.M. (1976) 'An investigation of Lorenz's babyishness', *Child Development* 7: 1191–3.
Gardner, B.T. and Wallach, L. (1965) 'Shapes of figures identified as a baby's head', *Perceptual and Motor Skills* 20: 135–42.
Groebel, J. and Hinde, R.A. (eds) (1989) *Aggression and War*, Cambridge: Cambridge University Press.
Heinroth, O. (1911) 'Beiträge zur Biologie, Namentlich Ethologie und Psychologie die Anatiden', *Verhandlungen 5. Internationale Ornithologische Kongress*, 589–702.
Hess, W.R. and Brügger, M. (1943) 'Das subkortikale Zentrum der affektiven Abwehrreaktion', *Helvetica Physiologica Acta* 1: 33–52.
Hinde, R.A. (1956) 'Ethological models and the concept of drive', *British Journal of the Philosophy of Science* 6: 321–31.
—— (1960) 'Energy models of motivation', *Symposia of the Society of Experimental Biology* 14: 199–213.
—— (1962) 'Some aspects of the imprinting problem', *Symposia of the Zoological Society of London* 8: 129–38.
—— (1968) 'Dichotomies in the study of development', in J.M. Thoday and A.S. Parkes (eds) *Genetic and Environmental Influences on Behaviour*, Edinburgh: Oliver and Boyd.
—— (1983) 'Ethology and child development,' in M.M. Haith and J. Campos (eds) *Mussen Handbook of Child Psychology. Vol. II*, New York: John Wiley.
Hinde, R.A. and Stevenson-Hinde, J. (eds) (1973) *Constraints on Learning*, London: Academic Press.
Holst, E. von and Mittelstaedt, H. (1950) 'Das Reafferenzprinzip', *Naturwissenschaften* 37: 464–76.
Horn, G. (1985) *Imprinting*, Oxford: Clarendon Press.
Huntingford, F.A. (1991) 'War and peace revisited', in M.S. Dawkins, T.R. Halliday and R. Dawkins (eds) *The Tinbergen Legacy*, London: Chapman and Hall.
Krebs, J.R. (1991) 'Animal communication: ideas derived from Tinbergen's activities', in M.S. Dawkins, T.R. Halliday and R. Dawkins (eds) *The Tinbergen Legacy*, London: Chapman and Hall.
Krebs, J.R. and Dawkins, R. (1984) 'Animal signals: mind reading and manipulation', in J.R. Krebs and N.B. Davies (eds) *Behavioural Ecology: An Evolutionary Approach*, Oxford: Blackwell.

104   *Robert A. Hinde*

Lehrman, D.S. (1953) 'A critique of Konrad Lorenz's theory of instinctive behaviour', *Quarterly Review of Biology* 28: 337–63.

—— (1970) 'Semantic and conceptual issues in the nature–nurture problem', in L.R. Aronson, E. Tobach, D. Lehrman and J. Rosenblatt (eds) *The Development and Evolution of Behaviour*, San Francisco: Freeman.

Lorenz, K. (1932) 'Betrachtungen über das Erkennen der arteigenen Triebhandlungen der Vögel', *Journal für Ornithologie* 80 (1).

—— (1935) 'Der Kumpan in der Umwelt des Vogels', *Journal für Ornithologie* 80 (2): 137–213; 289–413.

—— (1937) 'Über die Bildung des Instinktbegriffes', *Die Naturwissenschaften* 25 (19): 289–300; 307–18; 324–31.

—— (1941) 'Vergleichende Bewegungstudien an Anatinen', *Journal für Ornithologie* 89: 194–294.

—— (1950a) 'The comparative method in studying innate behaviour patterns', *Symposia of the Society of Experimental Biology* 4: 221–68.

—— (1950b) 'Part and parcel in animal and human societies', translated in K. Lorenz (1971) *Studies in Animal and Human Behaviour. Vol. II*, London: Methuen.

—— (1954) 'Psychology and phylogeny', translated in K. Lorenz (1971) *Studies in Animal and Human Behaviour. Vol. II*, London: Methuen.

—— (1958) 'Methods of approach to the problems of behaviour', translated in K. Lorenz (1971) *Studies in Animal and Human Behaviour. Vol. II*, London: Methuen.

—— (1961) 'Phylogenetische Anpassung und adaptive Modifikation des Verhaltens', *Festschrift für Tierpsychologie* 18: 139–87.

—— (1966a) *On Aggression*, London: Methuen.

—— (1966b) *Evolution and Modification of Behaviour*, London: Methuen.

—— (1970) 'The enmity between generations and its probable ethological causes', *Studium Generale* 23: 963–97.

—— (1978) *Vergleichende Verhaltensforschung: Grundlagen der Ethologie*, Vienna: Springer-Verlag.

McDougall, W. (1923) *An Outline of Psychology*, London: Methuen.

Maynard Smith, J. (1979) 'Game theory and the evolution of behaviour', *Proceedings of the Royal Society* 205: 474–88.

Maynard Smith, J. and Parker, G.A. (1976) 'The logic of asymmetrical contests', *Animal Behaviour* 24: 159–75.

Morris, D. (1967) *The Naked Ape*, London: Cape.

Moynihan, M.H. (1959) 'A revision of the family Laridae (Aves)', *American Museum Novitates* 1928: 1–42.

Oyama, S. (1985) *The Ontogeny of Information*, Cambridge: Cambridge University Press.

Rabbie, J. (1991) 'Determinants of instrumental intra-group cooperation', in R.A. Hinde and J. Groebel (eds) *Cooperation and Prosocial Behaviour*, Cambridge: Cambridge University Press.

Rawson, J. (1992) *The British Museum Book of Chinese Art*, London: British Museum Publication.

Rutter, M. (1992) 'A fresh look at maternal deprivation', in P. Bateson (ed.) *The Development and Integration of Behaviour*, Cambridge: Cambridge University Press.

Seligman, M.E.P. and Hager, J.L. (eds) (1972) *Biological Boundaries of Learning*, New York: Appleton-Century-Crofts.

Sternglanz, S.H., Gray, J.L. and Murakami, M. (1977) 'Adult preferences for infantile facial features', *Animal Behaviour* 25: 108–15.

Tajfel, H. (1978) Contributions in H. Tajfel (ed.) *Differentiation between Social Groups*, London: Academic Press.

Thorpe, W.H. (1961) *Bird Song*, Cambridge: Cambridge University Press.

Tinbergen, N. (1932 and 1935) 'Über die Orientierung der Bienenwolfes (*Philanthus triangulum* Fahr)', *Zeitschrift für vergleichende Physiologie* 16: 305–35 and 21: 699–716.

—— (1942) 'An objectivistic study of the innate behaviour of animals', *Bibliotheca Biotheoretica* 1: 39–98.

—— (1948) 'Social releasers and the experimental method required for their study', *Wilson Bulletin* 60: 6–51.

—— (1951) *The Study of Instinct*, Oxford: Clarendon Press.

—— (1952) 'Derived activities: their causation, biological significance, origin and emancipation during evolution', *Quarterly Review of Biology* 27: 1–32.

—— (1963) 'On the aims of methods of ethology', *Zeitschrift für Tierpsychologie* 20: 410–33.

—— (1968) 'On war and peace in animals and man', *Science* 160: 1411–18.

—— (1974) 'Ethology and stress diseases', *Science* 185: 20–7.

Tinbergen N. and Perdeck, A.C. (1950) 'On the stimulus situation releasing the begging response in the newly hatched herring gull chick (*Larus argentatus argentatus* Pont)', *Behaviour* 3: 1–39.

Tinbergen, N. and Tinbergen, E.A. (1983) *'Autistic' Children*, London: Allen and Unwin.

Tinbergen, N., Kruuk, H. and Paillette, M. (1962) 'Egg shell removal by the black-headed gull. *Larus r. ridibundus*, II', *Bird Study* 9: 123–51.

Weiss, P. (1941) 'Autonomous versus reflexogenous activity of the central nervous system', *Proceedings of the American Philosophical Society* 84: 53–64.

Whiting, B.B. and Whiting, J.W.M. (1975) *Children of Six Cultures*, Cambridge, Mass.: Harvard University Press.

Wuketits, F.M. (1990) *Konrad Lorenz: Leben und Werk eines grossen Naturforschers*, Munich: Piper.

Zahavi, A. (1975) 'Mate selection – a selection for handicap', *Journal of Theoretical Biology* 53: 205–14.

Plate 6 B.F. Skinner (1904–90)
By permission of D.E. Blackman

5   B.F. Skinner (1904–90)

Derek E. Blackman

B.F. Skinner was born on 20 March 1904 in Susquehanna, Pennsylvania, and died in Cambridge, Massachusetts, on 18 August 1990. He earned an AB (Bachelor of Arts) in English from Hamilton College, New York, in 1926, and at first intended to develop a career as a creative writer. However, he abandoned these plans and went instead to study psychology at Harvard University. He obtained his PhD there for a thesis on the history of the concept of the reflex and his own studies of animal learning. He continued at Harvard until 1936, and then took positions at the University of Minnesota (1936–45) and as chair of the department of psychology at the University of Indiana (1945–8). He returned to a chair of psychology at Harvard University in 1945, and was Edgar Pierce Professor of Psychology there from 1948 to 1957. He continued to work at Harvard as professor emeritus until just before his death at the age of 86.

Skinner wrote many books and papers over some sixty years, amongst which The Behavior of Organisms *(1938),* Science and Human Behavior *(1953),* Verbal Behavior *(1957) and* About Behaviorism *(1974) set forth his systematic approach to psychology, known as radical behaviourism or behaviour analysis. His novel* Walden Two *(1948) and* Beyond Freedom and Dignity *(1971) consider the implications of radical behaviourism in a broad societal context and are his most controversial works. His* Enjoying Old Age *(1983, written when Skinner was almost 80, with M.E. Vaughan) provides a down-to-earth account of being old. Skinner also wrote a three-volume autobiography:* Particulars of My Life *(1976);* The Shaping of a Behaviorist *(1979);* A Matter of Consequence *(1983).*

Skinner received many prestigious awards, including the Distinguished Scientific Award from the American Psychological Association (1958), the National Medal of Science, presented by President Johnson (1968), the International Award of the Joseph P. Kennedy Foundation for Mental Retardation (1971), the Humanist of the Year Award from the American Humanist Society (1972), the Award for Distinguished Contributions to Educational Research from the American Educational Research Association (1978), a Lifetime Achievement Award from the American Psychological Association (1990), and the William James Fellow Award of the American Psychological Society (1990). He was an honorary fellow of the British Psychological Society.

The members of the American Psychological Association are honored to recognize your lifetime of significant contributions to psychology and to the world.... As a pioneer in psychology, you challenged traditional ways of thinking.... As an intellectual leader, you enhance the stature of psychology and raise its intellectual climate to a higher level.... With great sensitivity to the human condition ... you laid the foundations for innovative applications of your work ... As a citizen of the world, you provide thoughtful, often provocative, and always compassionate insights into such uniquely human endeavors as ethics, freedom, dignity, governance, and peace.

(American Psychological Association 1990)

These words were included in a citation given to Burrhus Frederic Skinner by the American Psychological Association to celebrate his 'outstanding lifetime contribution to psychology'. This special award was given at a ceremony during the association's annual convention on 10 August 1990. Eight days later Fred Skinner was dead. Three days after that, an obituarist in the *Guardian* (Sutherland 1990) asked 'Why is it ... that Skinner is currently the psychologist who is best known to the general public and why was he so eminent in learned circles?'. The questions appear benign: the answers offered are not. First, 'he was a fanatic' and 'fanatics come to be believed, particularly if they . . . are completely convinced of their righteousness'. Second, 'early in life he made one important discovery' (namely that an animal's conditioned behaviour will survive the withdrawal of reward longer after intermittent rather than continuous reward). Third, 'he invented an ingenious automatic' experimental procedure which allowed an experimenter to 'scarper off to drink cups of coffee or play noughts and crosses with his colleagues'. This so-called Skinner Box, we are told, not for the first time, by this obituarist (and sadly, it has transpired not for the last), 'has been described as a bloodless method of decerebrating the animal', which 'some think . . . could be said of the effects of Skinnerian theory on his adherents'. Fourth, Skinner 'persisted' with his 'message' 'that it was possible to control everybody's behaviour by applying rewards and punishments in the right way'. It is conceded that 'some of [Skinner's] early work was important', but it is concluded 'that once he became the guru of psychology he severely held up progress in the subject'. Fortunately, it seems, 'his disciples are a dwindling band' in contemporary psychology.

The mismatch in content and tone in these two appraisals of Skinner and his work illustrate all too well Catania's (1988: 3) claim that 'of all contemporary psychologists B.F. Skinner is perhaps the most honored and the most maligned, the most widely recognised and the most misrepresented, the most cited and the most misunderstood'. When Hamlet lay dying, he said to his friend Horatio 'I am dead: thou livest; report me and my cause aright.' My hope in this chapter is to report Fred Skinner and his cause to you in what I hope is a fair, 'aright' manner, so that you may evaluate the man and his work alongside the other figures of intellectual stature in psychology who are included in this book. I should tell you at the outset that I have been a consistent advocate of Skinner's approach to psychology since I read psychology and philosophy for my first degree thirty years ago, and so I have now too often suffered the indignity of being termed one of his 'disciples'. As to the man, I did not know him well but I did correspond with him frequently and met him regularly, and I liked him.

In a short presentation such as this, it is hardly possible to provide a detailed exposition and evaluation of the work of a man who published some two hundred papers and books over a period of sixty years and who yet occupies such a charged position in the history of contemporary psychology. A bibliography of Skinner's works to 1988 is provided in Catania and Harnad (1988: 489–95), which also brings together some of his seminal (but technical) papers as prompts to many interesting commentaries and responses. Perhaps the barest indication of how Skinner's thinking developed is provided by listing some of the books which he published.

His first, *The Behavior of Organisms* (1938), is often still described as a classic work in experimental psychology. It consists largely of reports of studies of how the behaviour of rats reflects the environmental conditions to which they are exposed in laboratory experiments. These early studies in operant conditioning provided the basis for what has become a technically demanding and methodologically rigorous field of psychology known as the experimental analysis of behaviour. The book also contains considerable theoretical discussion: some points, such as Skinner's emphasis that 'operant' behaviour is emitted, not elicited by antecedent stimuli as was the 'respondent' behaviour studied by Pavlov, survived and found a central position in Skinner's subsequent theoretical analyses. Others tend to reflect the more transitory theoretical debates of the 1930s, the decade of grand learning theories in psychology, and they now seem dated.

Skinner's subsequent book *Science and Human Behavior* (1953) is an unusual and self-contained introductory review of what the field of psychology in its broadest sense could look like if Skinner's perspective were developed. Its chapters range from studies of operant conditioning, of course, through to behaviour in religious, political and economic domains. The book was a poor introduction to psychology (and indeed it still is), making little detailed contact with the research and ideas of other psychologists, but to the student of what has come to be called behaviour analysis it provides a provocative alternative agenda to that of more conventional psychological texts.

Verbal Behavior (Skinner 1957) occupies a unique position in the development of his thoughts and indeed in the history of psychology. Though Skinner himself believed this attempt to extend the principles of behaviour analysis from the animal laboratory to the understanding of the most complex aspects of human conduct to be his most important work, it was ill-fated. It became the butt of an alternative manifesto for the study of humanity, advocated by Chomsky (1959), whose lengthy, influential but ultimately ill-informed 'review' stole the attention of the academic community away from what Skinner was trying to say. Only now is the emphasis in psycholinguistics reorienting from the concepts of structure and linguistic competence to analyses of communicative performance within a pragmatic social world (see Andresen 1990).

About Behaviorism was published in 1974, when Skinner was already 70 years old: it presents the fundamentals of his approach to psychology and remains the most coherent, if somewhat defensive, exposition of general aspects of his behaviour-analytic approach in psychology. Finally in this non-chronological selective list of his books, Skinner wrote *Beyond Freedom and Dignity* (1971), which explores the implications of his approach to the study of behaviour for Western concepts of the autonomous person acting within society, upon which we build our system of morals and politics. This discussion is often within the context of concern for the survival of what Skinner saw as an increasingly precarious world. This book enraged many, who saw in it indications of illiberality and authoritarianism.

What are the emerging common threads in these and other works by Skinner? First and foremost is surely his emphasis on behaviour not as some kind of appendage to events 'at other levels', such as the mental or physiological, but rather as a natural phenomenon in its own right which is nested within an environmental or social context. Of course underlying physiological systems may be implicated in behaviour, as are cognitions, but even if they can be identified (which can be accomplished, according to Skinner, on the one hand by physiologists rather than by psychologists and on the other only by those who experience the private cognitions), there remains a need to understand the functional and dynamic relationships between behaviour and its context, and it is these relationships which are open to study by psychologists. If we can *understand* behaviour in terms of social context, such a focus may also suggest constructive ways of changing that social context with a view to producing desired changes in behaviour.

This idea is truly radical, but its force seems to me rarely to have been fully recognized by commentators and critics. For example, repeated descriptions of Skinner's system as 'mechanistic' or 'Newtonian' (e.g. Capra 1983: 181) are grossly misleading. To be sure, Skinner was bold in his commitment to determinism within psychology, the idea that what we do reflects *causal* influences which are open to study. This stance was based not, however, on explanations rooted in the metaphor of underlying machinery or mechanisms (either real or supposed) but on the functional relationships between behaviour and its environment. I have argued elsewhere (Blackman 1991) that in this respect Skinner's analyses, based though they are on principles abstracted from laboratory studies within an experimental biological tradition, in fact make substantial contact with modes of thought which have been described as social constructionist analyses of the so-called 'facts' of behaviour and experience (Table 5.1).

Table 5.1 Fields of behaviour analysis

Behaviour analysis
1 Experimental analysis of behaviour (operant conditioning)
2 Conceptual analysis (verbal behaviour; consciousness)
3 Applied behaviour analysis (education; clinic; social work; society)

Skinner's emphasis on the causal influences of environment on behaviour has been happily and persistently misunderstood by some. The claim has repeatedly been made that Skinner was a stimulus–response psychologist, although Skinner himself has repeatedly and explicitly denied this. The primary focus of his analysis is not to be found in the elicited reflexes of the kind studied by Pavlov, where behaviour may indeed aptly be described as the response or answer to some antecedent or goad. His focus was instead on what he termed emitted, or operant, behaviour: behaviour which does not appear to be prodded from an organism, but which nevertheless comes to occur at specifiable or predictable frequencies in certain environmental conditions. As has been noted before (Blackman 1980; Lee 1988), it is a pity that Skinner continued to use so freely in his writing the terms 'stimulus' and 'response', albeit modified explicitly or implicitly as 'discriminative and reinforcing stimuli' or 'operant responses'. This has surely contributed to the persistent misunderstandings of many of his critics, who seem to have believed that environmental influences on behaviour can only be interpreted as the prodding or the poking of mindless movements out of machines.

The true primary focus of Skinner's environmental analyses of behaviour is to be found, of course, in his analysis of reinforcement, the selection of a behavioural act by its consequences. This crucial aspect of Skinner's system has led to his being described as 'the Darwin of ontogeny' (Donahoe 1988). Darwin's theory of evolution, of course, supplanted purposive accounts of variations in taxonomic form: instead of interpreting species-characteristic taxonomic form as being designed to some end, the theory interprets it as being selected from variation by previous consequences in the phylogenetic past. So too with Skinner's theory of reinforcement: instead of interpreting our behaviour as reflecting some purpose, the theory interprets it as the result of selection by previous consequences in the past. This fundamental concept in his analysis is also, it seems, too easily misunderstood. For

Skinner, as he repeatedly explained, the concept of reinforcement in itself provided an explanation of current
behaviour, one which did not need to be supplemented by
accounts of mechanisms by which these events serve as
reinforcers. The focus is not on mechanisms internal to the
organisms or properties intrinsic to reinforcers, but rather
on the dynamic interplay between behaviour and context.
It is interesting that, according to Donahoe (1988), Darwin
frequently remarked on the special difficulties in understanding the force of the principle of natural selection that
seemed to be encountered by those trained in mathematics
and physical science, for 'the doctrine (of biological evolution) had dramatically called attention to the factor of
developmental change in the world, as physics and mathematics had previously exhibited the element of structural
constancy' (Morris 1962: ix). Perhaps it is no wonder, then,
in the light of the dominance in contemporary psychology
of so-called 'cognitive science', based as it is on the com-
putational metaphor and analogies between people and
machines, that this failure to understand the force of
Skinner's dynamic, contextualistic, selectionist account of
reinforcement continues too often to prevent a proper
understanding of his position.

The idea that current behaviour can be understood in
terms of selection by past reinforcement has gained much
empirical support from the detailed experimental analyses
of behaviour which have developed from Skinner's pioneering studies of the conditioning of operant behaviour in rats.
These studies have benefited from the apparatus developed
by Skinner in his own experimental work. Although I have
seen it claimed in an undergraduate essay that he
'discovered the Skinner Box', Skinner in fact of course
invented or created this apparatus (which he disliked
having named after him by others) in which the effects of
contingencies of reinforcement on the behaviour of animals
could be studied in a controlled manner. These experimental arrangements are abstractions of the world in which our
behaviour might be thought to be influenced by environmental events. The animals who adapt well to laboratory

life 'stand for' behaving organisms in general, including us. Arbitrary patterns of behaviour which these animals may emit frequently or rarely and which may be readily recorded by the experimenter, such as lever pressing by rats or key pecking by pigeons, 'stand for' operant behaviour in general, those patterns of behaviour which are emitted within a surrounding environmental or social context. Environmental events, such as the presentation of lights, sounds, food, etc., 'stand for' those events in non-structured situations which may function as discriminative stimuli, setting the occasion for behaviour to occur, or as reinforcers, acting to select out patterns of behaviour which they follow.

Thus a powerful laboratory model has emerged which has added very considerable subtlety and complexity to our understanding of the importance of the environmental context for behaviour. We now know that the detailed characteristics of current behavioural repertoires result not just from the fact that reinforcers have followed behaviour in the past, but also from the detailed relationships between the behaviour and reinforcers, the so-called contingencies or schedules of reinforcement. Similarly, experimental studies have shown how the influence on behaviour of reinforcers can be modulated by circumstances which are differentially associated with the presentation of reinforcers, the so-called discriminative control of behaviour. Thus has emerged a subtle and complex elaboration in behaviour analysis of the so-called three-term contingency (a:b:c): in some circumstances (a) behavioural acts (b) occur as a result of the selective effects in the past of their consequences (c). The reinforcers which follow that behaviour in those circumstances, and the precise frequency and patterning of the behaviour at different times, reflect the details of the various relationships within this three-term contingency.

Because of the nature of Skinner's own earlier experimental work, and because it has spawned so many experimental studies of conditioned behaviour in animals, Skinner is often depicted as a white-coated laboratory scientist. Furthermore, the contingencies of reinforcement, whose effects on behaviour have been so extensively studied in operant conditioning experiments, demand sophisticated apparatus to control environmental events and to record behaviour. So the white-coated scientist may be depicted standing in front of elaborate switching and timing devices or even expensive computers (if, of course, the opportunity has been resisted to scarper off to drink coffee!). Thus emerges an icon of cold scientific objectivity and a ruthless science of rats' behaviour, extrapolation from which may appear threatening and demeaning. If scientists now have ways of controlling the apparently voluntary behaviour of their charges, what havoc might they wreak when they direct their menacing techniques to the control of *our* behaviour? What experimental conditions might they seek to make us endure?

But of course we are not rats, and our worlds are not controlled by scientists. We are agents, interacting with each other within the ebb and flow of the everyday social discourse we construct. It is not the experimental techniques which Skinner sought to extrapolate from the laboratory to 'make us behave'. Rather it is the radical and provocative conceptualization of behaviour as a naturally occurring phenomenon explicable in terms of its context which Skinner sought to extend from these detailed laboratory studies into our (and his) everyday worlds of social interaction. Lee (1988: 170) has described this as a 'conceptual shift from an organocentric psychology to a psychology of action'.

In truth the balance of Skinner's extensive writings in the psychological literature is certainly not to be found in the output of white-coated scientific technology but in the humane discussion of the implications of his way of looking at behaviour for the human condition. Contrary to the popular image, Skinner wrote far more about the behaviour of humans than of rats, and far more about trying to understand its dynamics than trying to manipulate or change it. A key step in this progression is to be found in his seminal work *Verbal Behavior* (1957).

Verbal Behavior is an exercise of interpretation in which Skinner sought to extend the interpretative principles emerging from the experimental analysis of behaviour to that most complex of human behavioural repertoires, language. He tried to move away from the conventional view that what we say reflects some underlying meaning or communicative intention, interpreting even this in terms of its dynamic relationships with its (social) environment, or as a function of its social context. Skinner did not thereby assume that contingencies of reinforcement within this social context need to be contrived as they are in the conditioning laboratory. Nor did he assume that they are unidirectional: in everyday life, the behaviour emitted by one person may serve to reinforce that emitted by another, and in turn the behaviour of the latter may have selective reinforcing effects on the behaviour of the former. Skinner attempted to develop a way of looking even at speech, even at what we 'choose' to say, in terms of social contingencies of reinforcement within these dynamic reciprocal interactions. At its simplest, his thesis is that our social community can be said to select and tune our verbal utterances through processes of social reinforcement and discriminative control whose fundamental dynamics have been explored within the experimental analysis of behaviour. This leads to analyses of classes of speech acts which may be differentiated in terms of their relationships to surrounding contingencies of reinforcement. For example, mands are said to be speech acts (classes of behaviour) which are followed by characteristic consequences, while tacts are speech acts which are socially reinforced when emitted in the presence of an object or event, or of some property of an object or event. This exercise in the interpretation of verbal behaviour by Skinner is long, detailed and technically demanding. I have already noted that it had sadly little impact on the development of psychology. Chomsky's hostile review, to which Skinner did not respond, no doubt contributed to some of the persistent misrepresentations of his system, for example that it is based on stimulus–response accounts or that reinforcers have properties other than their selective effects on behaviour. The crucial links between Skinner's account of verbal behaviour and his

analysis of experience, or 'private events', have therefore
also remained unnoticed by many critics who assert that
Skinner's system has no place for thoughts and experience.

In fact, far from pretending that people have no inner
lives or experience (who could be so silly?), Skinner was
one of the few psychologists to have addressed openly some
of the fundamental questions of the provenance and
functions of consciousness. For example, he included in the
functional class of tacts verbal behaviour which relates not
only to the external world but also to feelings or experience.
He argued that because the latter cannot be explicitly
monitored or observed by the verbal community in the
direct way that we can monitor physical events, they cannot enter so precisely into the social dynamics of
discriminative control and reinforcement. However, the
social community gives its best approximation to what
might be deemed appropriate reinforcement of statements
about private events, for example by seeking observable
circumstances which imply the statement is likely to be
made under 'appropriate' discriminative control. In this
way, Skinner argues, the verbal community generates
awareness by teaching us to describe our past and present
behaviour and the variables of which it is a function. Thus
consciousness itself is said by Skinner to be a 'social
product', which emerges from social interaction within a
verbal community.

Skinner's frequent discussions of these matters surely
refute any claim that his theoretical system has no place
for experience within it. However, what is clear is that the
role of experience differs markedly in his system from that
which we conventionally assign to it. For example, it is common to interpret overt behaviour as a reflection of private
experience, as if the latter is somehow an autonomous cause
of what we do. In Skinner's system, on the other hand,
private experience is not itself uncaused, but instead reflects
social interactions in the same way as does overt behaviour
(Skinner would say 'other' behaviour). This dynamic and
essentially social view of mental life makes considerable

contact with social constructionist theories, though I have argued that the image of Skinner the white-coated biological scientist has deflected intellectual attention away from this important point (see Blackman 1991).

In an effort to capture the essential features of Skinner's systematic approach to psychology in a few words, I realize I have been forced to present challenging and unconventional views in an abstract and unelaborated manner. I cannot hope here to represent in self-contained and persuasive detail ideas that Skinner himself laboured to discuss repeatedly and at length throughout the last forty years of his life. But perhaps enough has been said here at least to challenge some of the more serious and persistent misattributions of Skinner's critics, for example that his is the psychology of the puppeteer, that it seeks somehow to reduce the complexities of human behaviour to simple repetitive patterns of behaviour by rats and pigeons, that it crassly denies the reality and importance of experience. In trying to present the essence of Skinner's cause aright, I have tried to emphasize its essential social dynamism. Behaviour is thought to be constructed by its social context, through principles of selection by reinforcers and modulation by discriminative control, rather than as some appendage to processes operating at some other level within us. Such a view does not restrict us to simplistic stimulus–response analyses. Nor does it deny the special importance of that crucial and unique attribute, language. This too, however, is interpreted as a function of social contingencies of reinforcement, and is seen by Skinner as a key to the development of private experience and self-awareness, which are thus also interpreted as products of our interactions with our social world rather than as entities within us which serve as autonomous causes of our overt behaviour.

Persistent, perhaps wilful, oversimplifications and misrepresentations of Skinner's thought have severely blunted its impact, both within and beyond the confines of psychology itself. One reason for this is perhaps to be found in Skinner's readiness to consider the practical and societal implications of his concept of the behaving person. It is clear that his boldness has led some to see him as an illiberal authoritarian advocate of the application of a psychological technology which can be used to control the behaviour of others. For example, Skinner's views led him to a distinctively active stance with respect to the 'professional' applications of behaviour analysis in education and clinic. He argued (e.g. 1966) that the goals of education should be expressed in concrete behavioural terms, that educational programmes should be carefully designed in a logical sequence which arranges successive approximations to the targets, that pupils should work individually and at their own pace in such a way that the successful completion of each step in a programme might be followed by potentially reinforcing consequences such as confirmation of correctness. Before the introduction of today's computer-based educational technology, which often in fact incorporates many of these principles, Skinner advocated the development of teaching programmes which could be used in mechanical 'teaching machines'. Although Skinner argued that this systematization of learning would release the teacher to monitor and improve the effectiveness of the steps of a programme and to engage in personal interaction with the pupils as an educational manager rather than as the font of wisdom, the idea of teaching machines as the base of programmed learning appeared to some to be unduly restrictive and lacking in social context. An austere image was thereby established, although Keller (1968) has incorporated Skinner's philosophy and principles in non-automated study programmes (personalized self-instruction) which maximize social interactions for successful progress through the various steps.

A similarly austere image was associated with early attempts to use principles of behavioural analysis in the context of clinical psychology. A theoretical system which interprets behaviour as a reflection of its social context readily gives rise to the idea that behaviour change may be produced by changing the dynamics of social reinforcement and discriminative control. The techniques of 'behaviour modification', in which these reinforcement contingencies were manipulated in order to produce behavioural change in patients with a mental illness or mental handicap, appeared to be encouragingly successful, but some critics were concerned about the ways in which these programmes were imposed on clients by behaviour modifiers, giving rise to suggestions that they (and Skinner) were manipulative or coercive. Such concerns gained further force when the objective of an intervention was said to be not the conventional cure of an underlying disease or pathology but rather the development of specific behaviours, and when so many of the initial clients were institutionalized and relatively inarticulate. However, the techniques of behaviour modification have over the years gradually been extended to ever more complex and less constrained circumstances and client groups, as, for example, in social work, and principles of so-called 'contingency contracting' have been used to negotiate both desirable goals and acceptable methods for interventions with articulate clients.

In fact the field of applied behaviour analysis is now a well-established feature of applied psychology in general. The techniques of behavioural change based on concepts of reinforcement and discriminative control in a social context are widely used, though sometimes, it must be conceded, in a somewhat pragmatic or cook-book manner which makes little contact with the way of interpreting behaviour problems as social products that is intrinsic to Skinner's behaviour-analytic perspective. In my view such a pragmatic approach is more likely to lead to insensitive programmes, for interventions rooted in behaviour-analytic interpretations will always see behaviour as a reflection of the contingencies of reinforcement, and thus attribute responsibility for shortcomings or problems in a programme to the programme, while the more pragmatic approach may continue to attribute responsibility for any problems to the client, despite the programme of intervention.

In general the techniques of applied behaviour analysis have been advocated by and entrusted to psychological professionals, though increasingly the priority of psychologists in this regard has been challenged by teachers, nurses, psychiatrists and social workers. Society has, therefore, been able to look to professional monitoring to ensure that acceptable methods have been used in an effort to achieve appropriate goals, though this has not always remained uncontroversial. A more general and more exposed challenge to traditional Western conceptions of the person in society is to be found in Skinner's extrapolations of the principles of behaviour analysis to the everyday world in which we all live. His interest in these matters can be traced from his novel *Walden Two* (1948), an account of a fictional Utopia in which the social needs of the community are identified and the social contingencies adjusted in the context of plans to achieve those needs. There is undoubtedly an element of autobiography in this novel, in so far as the fictional characters often express views which are clearly those of Skinner himself. Many critics have claimed more, that the central figure in the planned community, Frazier, plays a role which Skinner himself aspired to, namely the ultimate and autonomous controller of others, although (like any sensitive manager who does not resort to aversive methods of control) Frazier's behaviour is as enmeshed in the social context of Walden Two as is the behaviour of others.

Skinner's *Beyond Freedom and Dignity* (1971) provides an elaborated discussion of the socio-political implications of his behaviour-analytic stance, and not surprisingly it is this book which has proved to be his most controversial work. Although it has been described as a 'blueprint of hell', it is in truth an analysis of the ultimate implications of the idea that our behaviour can be interpreted as a function of our social context rather than as some appendage to underlying processes. Skinner argues that our traditional concepts of freedom and autonomy of action deflect us from recognizing the influences of social reinforcers on our own behaviour. Furthermore, our emphasis on the dignity of people, on how 'they' may be held responsible for 'their' behaviour, blamed or praised for 'their' actions, is no more than a reflection of our ignorance of the social dynamics which give rise to that behaviour. Skinner is not suggesting that behaviour *should* be controlled, but rather that our literature of freedom and dignity deflects us from recognizing that it *is* controlled by social dynamics. He did not argue that aversive procedures should be imposed on others (in any case, he argued again and again that aversive procedures do not in fact work effectively in producing sustainable behavioural change). Indeed, Skinner did not argue that *any* contingencies of reinforcement should be imposed on others. Instead he suggested that the concepts of autonomy and freedom deflect us from recognizing how our behaviour is influenced, particularly if that influence results from positive reinforcement rather than from aversive procedures. The focus of his discussion was therefore on the dynamics of social interactions within a community. In particular he discussed how imbalances of influence within such interactions, which too easily remain unilluminated by the seachlight beam which directs our attention to the concept of personal freedom, give rise to moral problems. Skinner's concept of society is certainly not one which addresses the imposition of the will of some authoritarian leader on the behaviour of others by means of coercive methods. Instead he argues that the needs of a society will be better met if they are expressed in concrete, precise terms and the interactive flux of social dynamics is recognized in relation to those needs.

In this brief review I have tried merely to indicate the range of topics within psychology which was addressed by Skinner. It is true that he developed experimental techniques for studying the influences of environmental events on the behaviour of animals. It is true too, as Skinner himself came publicly to regret, that he illustrated the power of these techniques, for example by teaching pigeons to play ping-pong. The impact of the behaviour technology which has flowed from his pioneering studies can hardly be overstated. Indeed, if society is looking to a science of psychology to produce an effective technology of behavioural change, the technology arising from Skinner's scientific work is by far the most obvious, wide-ranging and effective so far. But the true significance of Skinner's work is to be found, I believe, in the systematic perspective or philosophy for which his experimental studies provided an underpinning, the idea that behaviour is a naturally occurring phenomenon which can be explained and understood in contextualistic terms, as a dynamic function of the social environment with which it interacts. This led Skinner to a view of what a person is, the question surely at the heart of psychology, which is radically different from the predominant Western view. In trying to capture the essence of this idea, Baer (1976: see also Hineline 1980) has described the person in behaviour-analytic terms not as the ultimate and autonomous cause of behaviour but as its *host*: the living organism is in a sense a place where behaviour results from phylogenetic influences and social contingencies of reinforcement coming together. I may have been too bold in trying to capture even the shadow of this challenging idea in a short presentation such as this, but for me it is this philosophical challenge (derived as it may be from detailed empirical experiments) which justifies the inclusion of Skinner in a list of intellectual forces in the historical development of psychology. Much of Skinner's own work was devoted not to experimental analyses of environmental influences on behaviour in the animal laboratory but to discussions of the implications of his conception of the person and behaviour in a range of contexts. His radical theoretical analyses of human verbal behaviour formed the crucial step in this process, leading as they did to discussions of consciousness and its place in psychology which make contact with the currently modish ideas of such psychologists as Vygotsky. Although experimental studies of the effects on behaviour of consequences of reinforcement provide an underpinning for technological applications in professional practice, the implications of Skinner's theoretical position are developed in their most challenging form in discussions of the behaviour of individuals in society, an analysis which brings to the fore the moral and indeed political issues which, in general, psychologists have been perhaps too reluctant to confront in developing their discipline.

But what of Skinner the man? In presentations such as this it is conventional to begin by describing the biographical details of the person whose work is to be discussed. On this occasion I have chosen to revert to those details. Perhaps this is because I want to end on a human note rather than on what some critics see as an inhumane philosophy. But my own history tells me that the attitude to the person can become tainted by attitudes to the ideas: I have on several occasions been introduced by well-meaning hosts as a behaviourist but quite a nice person. I did not, of course, fail to notice or appreciate the compliment: but why the 'but'? I had never heard a parallel introduction, as, for example, of the developmental, social or cognitive scientist *but* (or even *and*) a nice person. In the case of Skinner, I detect an expectation on the part of many that the eccentricities of the man will be weaknesses, that any personal strengths will be threatening to others. But, though he had his foibles (as do we all), I found him a serious scholar and a kindly man, one who applied his perspective to his interactions with others and to his understanding of himself.

Fred Skinner was raised in a small Pennsylvania town, Susquehanna. Though he may have become one of the most famous of psychologists, I found nobody when I visited the town sixty years later who knew of him. But I could reconstruct from the first part of his autobiography (Skinner 1976) many 'particulars' of his childhood, for his own account of his early life is full of stories about everyday social interactions which shaped his behaviour rather than of grand interpretations of what many might seek to call his psychological development. Skinner went in 1922 to Hamilton College to read English: he tells us that he wanted to be a creative writer, and indeed Robert Frost encouraged him at one time by remarking that he was capable of 'real niceties of observation' (Skinner 1979: 249). But his attempts to develop this interest were unsuccessful, because, as Skinner said, he found he had nothing to say.

After he had subsequently turned to the study of psychology, Skinner gave up playing the saxophone because it seemed to him at the time to be 'the wrong instrument for a psychologist'. When asked late in life how he bore the strain of being so widely misunderstood, he replied: 'I find that I need to be understood only three or four times a year.' I choose these anecdotes to illustrate a self-deprecating style which often characterized the man.

Skinner's career in academic psychology also could not be said to be one of self-aggrandizement. From the time he began his graduate studies till his death he largely worked at Harvard University without the support of any extended team. While accepting honours such as the US National Medal of Science in 1968 and a Kennedy Foundation Award in 1971, he avoided positions of power and influence within his university and within the psychological community. His personal life was quiet, drawing strength from a marriage of more than fifty years to Eve, with whom he had two daughters, one of whom is now an educationist and the other an artist. Skinner's deep academic and personal friendship with his graduate student colleague Fred Keller also flourished for more than fifty years.

Skinner was intensely fond of music, and was always fascinated by gadgets. The development of the so-called Skinner Box for the study of operant conditioning surely reflects this latter interest, as did his forays into teaching machines. It led him also into developing an air-crib, in truth no more than an air-conditioned and temperature-controlled cot for his second daughter, in which she was placed unconstrained by clothes at the times when other children are wrapped in clothes and placed in a conventional crib. The 'clang' between the gadget and the so-called Skinner Box prompted malicious stories about how Skinner had brought his child up in a box and the dire effects this was said to have had on her, neither of which was in any sense true but neither of which has been affected by the facts. Skinner's office was, however, justifiably famous for its gadgetry, with eccentric labour-saving and other devices designed to overcome the niggles which most of us learn to live with.

Skinner *was* an unusual person in many ways. For example, there are endless stories about how available he made himself to any who wanted to talk to him, however junior. As an advocate of the effectiveness of positive reinforcement rather than aversive procedures, he was famed for 'not noticing' behaviour in others which he did not seek to encourage while responding to that which he did want to strengthen. This trait may have contributed to the relative neglect of some of his writing: for example, he never responded to Chomsky's destructive review of his account of verbal behaviour, explaining later that he disliked the stridency of the review and decided that it was not really about the ideas in his book, but this may have done no more than encourage some to think that he was not able to resist Chomsky's onslaught (see MacCorquodale 1969). Similarly Skinner invariably dealt with frequent harsh misrepresentations and even malicious *ad hominem* criticism with calm and (may I say it?) dignity, though I am sure that many hurt him. Skinner was also alert to the environmental circumstances which influenced his own behaviour, and he worked in a somewhat ritualized manner in order to maximize these influences, to help 'make' behaviour happen that achieved the clear goals which he set himself.

I find it hard to see Skinner as the authoritarian bigot that some have made him out to be. No doubt that reflects the contingencies of reinforcement inherent in my interactions with him. Nor do I see his writing as simplistic, demeaning or manipulative, as I have tried to show by my brief discussion.

I want to end with some comments made by Jerome Bruner, doyen of a very different approach to psychology from that advocated by Skinner. Bruner wrote:

We crossed swords on most of the central theoretical issues in psychology. Yet in all our years of colleague-ship at Harvard and after, I never doubted his goodwill, his sincerity, or his eagerness to do fair battle over ideas.

128   Derek E. Blackman

He was as civilized in his dealings with the world as he was passionate in his Utopian convictions about how it should eventually conduct itself. One can only be grateful for such an honorable opponent.

(Mahoney 1991: 634)

I am grateful to have had this opportunity to offer Skinner's life and intellectual work to you as one example of psychology's strivings to understand a little better the mysteries of behaviour and of mind. His is an approach worthy of consideration, I believe, for, as Leo Baker of Trinity College, Dublin (1990: 94), has suggested, Skinner advocated 'a Copernican shift in our theorising about the nature of human behaviour', by moving from 'the "centrism" of humans being initiators of their own behaviour' to a position in which 'the onus of provenance [rests on] the surrounding environment, past and present'. Skinner's contributions to intellectual life and to psychology are challenging and deserve to be considered more carefully and with more sympathy than has generally been the case in recent years. It is therefore pleasing to be able to end this brief review by reference to the recent publication of a scholarly but generous reappraisal of Skinner's work by Richelle (1993).

REFERENCES

American Psychological Association (1990) 'Citation for outstanding lifetime contribution to psychology: B.F. Skinner', *American Psychologist* 45: 1205.
Andresen, J. (1990) 'Skinner and Chomsky 30 years later or: the return of the repressed', *Historiographica Linguistica* 17: 145–166 (reprinted in *The Behavior Analyst* [1991] 14: 49–60).
Baer, D.M. (1976) 'The organism as host', *Human Development* 19: 87–98.
Baker, L. (1990) 'Obituary for B.F. Skinner', *Irish Psychologist* (November).
Blackman, D.E. (1980) 'Images of man in contemporary behaviourism', in A.J. Chapman and D.M. Jones (eds) *Models of Man*, Leicester and London: British Psychological Society and Macmillan.
—— (1991) 'B.F. Skinner and G.H. Mead: on biological science and social science', *Journal of the Experimental Analysis of Behavior* 55: 251–65.

Capra, F. (1983) *The Turning Point: Science, Society and the Rising Culture*, London: Fontana.

Catania, A.C. (1988) 'The operant behaviorism of B.F. Skinner', in A.C. Catania and S. Harnad (eds) *The Selection of Behavior: The Operant Behaviorism of B.F. Skinner: Comments and Consequences*, Cambridge: Cambridge University Press.

Catania, A.C. and Harnad, S. (eds) (1988) *The Selection of Behavior: The Operant Behaviorism of B.F. Skinner: Comments and Consequences*, Cambridge: Cambridge University Press.

Chomsky, N. (1959) 'A review of Skinner's *Verbal Behavior*', *Language* 35: 26–58.

Donahoe, J.W. (1988) 'Skinner: the Darwin of ontogeny?', in A.C. Catania and S. Harnad (eds) *The Selection of Behavior: The Operant Behaviorism of B.F. Skinner: Comments and Consequences*, Cambridge: Cambridge University Press.

Hineline, P.N. (1980) 'The language of behavior analysis: its community, its functions, and its limitations', *Behaviorism* 8: 67–86.

Keller, F.S. (1968) 'Goodbye, teacher . . . ', *Journal of Applied Behavior Analysis* 1: 79–89.

Lee, V.L. (1988) *Beyond Behaviorism*, Hillsdale, NJ: Erlbaum.

MacCorquodale, K. (1969) 'B.F. Skinner's *Verbal Behavior*: a retrospective appreciation', *Journal of the Experimental Analysis of Behavior* 12: 831–41.

Mahoney, M.J. (1991) 'B.F. Skinner: a collective tribute', *Canadian Psychology* 32: 628–35.

Morris, C.W. (1962) 'George H. Mead as social psychologist and social philosopher', in *G.H. Mead: Mind, Self and Society: From the Standpoint of a Social Behaviorist*, Chicago: Chicago University Press.

Richelle, M.N. (1993) *B.F. Skinner: A Reappraisal*, Hove: Erlbaum.

Skinner, B.F. (1938) *The Behavior of Organisms: An Experimental Analysis*, New York: Appleton-Century-Crofts.

—— (1948) *Walden Two*, New York: Macmillan.

—— (1953) *Science and Human Behavior*, New York: Macmillan.

—— (1957) *Verbal Behavior*, New York: Appleton-Century-Crofts.

—— (1966) *The Technology of Teaching*, New York: Appleton-Century-Crofts.

—— (1971) *Beyond Freedom and Dignity*, New York: Alfred A. Knopf.

—— (1974) *About Behaviorism*, New York: Alfred A. Knopf.

—— (1976) *Particulars of My Life*, New York: Alfred A. Knopf.

—— (1979) *The Shaping of a Behaviorist*, New York: Alfred A. Knopf.

Sutherland, N.S. (1990) 'Fanatical guru of behaviourism (Obituary of B.F. Skinner)', *Guardian*, 21 August.

Plate 7 Jean Piaget (1896–1980)
By permission of Blackstar

6 Jean Piaget (1896–1980)

Peter E. Bryant

Jean Piaget was born in Neuchâtel, Switzerland, in 1896. As a boy he showed brilliant promise in zoology, publishing his first scientific paper at the age of 10. By the age of 15, several articles on molluscs had gained him a reputation amongst European zoologists.

After completing a doctorate in zoology at the University of Neuchâtel, he went to Zurich where he studied psychiatry at Eugen Bleuler's clinic under both Bleuler and Carl Jung. He then went to work at the Sorbonne in Paris for two years, during which time he carried out research with Simon, who had earlier collaborated with Binet. Piaget was given the task of trying out new intellectual tests with children and became interested in the reasoning which they adopted to solve these tasks and how this reasoning changed with age. This experience was the starting point for his long time pursuit of the empirical study of the development of children's thinking, for which he developed a quasi-clinical method. The method involved a careful questioning of the subject during the course of an experimental procedure and much of his early work was based on such observation and experiment carried out on his two daughters.

With his theory of intellectual development, Piaget sought to make a contribution to a discipline he helped found: genetic epistemology (originally named by the American psychologist J.M. Baldwin). Genetic epistemology is interdisciplinary, concerned with the nature and origins of human knowledge and drawing upon philosophy, biology and cybernetics, as well as psychology.

On his return to Switzerland, he was made Director of the Institut Jean Jacques Rousseau, and later (1929) became Professor of Child Psychology at the University of Geneva. In 1955 he founded the International Centre of Genetic Epistemology in Geneva and became its director. He was actively involved in UNESCO and, until his retirement in 1975, was co-director of the International Bureau of Education.

During his career he produced more than 50 books and a very great number of scientific papers. His work has had a wide and continuing impact on psychology, education, linguistics and physics. He died in 1980.

I think that it is fair to say that there are currently three clearly different approaches to the study of the development of intelligent behaviour. Each has its enthusiastic supporters and its critics, and each has produced some notable contributions to our knowledge of children's intelligence. One of these approaches, a relatively recent arrival on the scene, denies that there is much intellectual development – at any rate in any deep sense (Gelman and Gallistel 1978; Spelke *et al.* 1992; Starkey *et al.* 1990; Johnson and Morton 1991). The people who take this view agree that some quite remarkable changes take place in children's behaviour as they grow older, but argue that these are changes mainly on the surface. There is no deep change, they claim: children are born with most of their fundamental intellectual capacities intact and their main task in childhood is to learn how to deploy these intellectual mechanisms effectively.

Another approach, which in its modern form can be traced back to the ideas of the great Russian psychologist, Lev Vygotsky (Vygotsky 1986; van der Veer and Valsiner 1991), is to look to culture. Vygotsky argued that children are born with considerable intellectual abilities but that they have to come to terms with the inventions and discoveries of the sophisticated culture into which they are born, and that what they learn about these cultural achievements will transform their intellectual processes. Thus learning to read, to count, to navigate and, to take a more recent example, to use computers are achievements in themselves, but they also have a considerable effect on the child's intellectual processes. These so-called 'cultural tools' become part of their intellectual repertoire.

There is a third approach which we owe almost entirely to the remarkable work of an old sparring partner of

Vygotsky's – Jean Piaget. It is that children are born bereft of intellectual mechanisms, and that before they can come to grips with the culture in which they live, before they can understand the environment around them, they have to acquire for themselves a set of intellectual mechanisms which allows them to be logical, to organize their thoughts and experiences in an orderly way and eventually to reflect on their own intellectual processes. It is this acquisition of intellectual mechanisms that paces human development, that determines when children will understand properly the words that they hear and even some of the words that they speak, when they will grasp even the most rudimentary elements of the arithmetic, science, geography and history which they hear about every day at school.

The facts of Jean Piaget's life and work are simple, but dramatic. His great work started when, as a young and already successful biologist, he asked himself the question 'How do we gain knowledge and understanding of the world around us?' His answer to that question took the form of fifty years' unremitting research on children and speculation about children, and during that time he produced the most ingenious and original set of experiments and the most powerful theory that have ever been known in developmental (that is to say, child) psychology. His experiments are certainly the most frequently repeated developmental experiments that there are and his theory, controversial though it has been, is still the starting point and often the end point as well for most work on children's intellectual growth.

Piaget's interest in children began with a visit in the 1920s to Paris. There he spent some time working with Simon – Binet's collaborator in the construction of the first successful intelligence test. Simon asked Piaget to try out a new sub-test which had been devised in England by Cyril Burt. In this test children were asked questions of the sort 'Jane is fairer than Sue, Sue is fairer than Ellen. Who is fairer, Jane or Ellen?' Burt's intention in posing these inferential questions was to find another way to predict and measure individual children's intellectual capacity, but

Piaget (1921) was struck by a very different thought when he saw the way young children react to such problems. He found, as Burt had found before him, that these particular inferences – they are called transitive inferences because they involve transitive relations along a quantity continuum – are strikingly difficult for young children to make. Yet they involve a form of reasoning which lies at the heart of some fundamental forms of intellectual understanding. If you cannot make a transitive inference, Piaget argued, then you cannot really work out the ordinal relations in any continuum: so you will not understand that if 3 is more than 2 and 2 more than 1 then 3 must be more than 1. Nor can you understand how measurement works, for both transitive inferences and measurement involve taking a common measure (B) to compare two or more quantities (A and C) which cannot be directly compared with each other (Piaget *et al.* 1960). If children of 6, 7 and 8 years really cannot make or understand transitive inferences, as Piaget immediately claimed, there will be much that is obscure for them in their initial maths lessons. This logical gap should also lead to difficulties with spatial relationships, according to Piaget. He argued quite convincingly that in order to understand spatial dimensions like horizontality and verticality, we have to be able to link separate spatial comparisons (the water level in a tilted glass is parallel to the table; the table top is parallel to the floor; the floor is parallel to the water level; therefore they are all in the same orientation), and to coordinate comparisons in this way is in effect to make a series of transitive inferences (Piaget and Inhelder 1963).

I dwelt on the story of Piaget's work and views on transitive inferences partly because this was his first study of young children but mainly because it illustrates very clearly what was to become the main theme of his life work – that children are born without logic, that in the following years they have to construct for themselves a logical framework, and that their capacity to understand their world and to learn about it are entirely constrained by the pace of this slow but inexorable logical development.

Let us turn now to a brief summary of Piaget's account of children's intellectual development. I should like to begin it with the remark that Piaget's theory – and every other decent developmental theory – has two parts to it. One is an account of what it is that changes during childhood – what is the difference between a child of 4 months and a 1-year-old, what changes between the ages of 3 years and 5 years, and so on. As we have already seen, Piaget's claim here is that logic develops, and thus that children become more logical as they grow older.

The second aspect of Piaget's theory is a very clear claim about the causes of developmental change. Any theory that argues for radical changes during childhood must also make some statement about what makes these changes happen. Piaget conscientiously provided such a statement. In brief, his central claim here was that children construct their own intellectual development for themselves on their own and largely as a result of their informal experiences with the environment. As we shall see, one of the most important aspects of this causal claim is that of what does not cause development. Children do not change just as a result of being taught about how the world works: nor do they change as a result of the activity of pre-programmed innate mechanisms. Children change because they are drawn into experiences which make them change their view of the world again and again. They work it out for themselves (Piaget 1973).

Nearly all of Piaget's actual empirical research dealt with the first of these two questions. He started with one instance – the transitive inference – of perfectly normal children apparently fumbling with an intellectual move that to any adult seems transparently simple, and he continued in the same way. Right through this work there is an air of frank astonishment at the radical differences between young children and adults and between children of different ages.

We should start with his ideas about infants. Piaget (1952b) claimed that infants are born with the capacity to produce certain movements and simple patterns of behaviour, such as grasping and sucking and following moving objects visually, but with nothing much else. His main claim about these few rudimentary actions was not that they are elementary, but that they are uncoordinated. This in turn means that the baby has no inkling of herself as a physical entity – no idea where she leaves off and the world outside starts – and thus no understanding of herself as a physical entity surrounded by other physical entities, some of which are inanimate and others not.

Piaget came to this view on the basis of some meticulous observations of the way in which children learn over the first four to five months to reach for things which they can see. At first, Piaget observed, there seems to be no coordination at all between what they look at and see and what they do. After two months the child will look at her hand as it swims by in her visual field, but apparently in much the same way as she looks at her mother or the cat going by. According to Piaget the child has no way at all of realizing that her hand is part of her and the cat is not. The next small step is that the child does begin to arrest her hand and look at it when it comes into her visual field. Piaget's view is that this happens at first by chance: the child happens to produce the command 'stop' on one occasion when the hand is in the visual field and discovers that this produces an interesting visual result, which she tries to repeat later on. Presumably she tries to repeat it at first as much when the cat goes by as when her own hand does, but only the hand stops, which gives the child the first clue that she is a separate entity surrounded by other independent entities.

The next step in this intriguing process is that inevitably while the child is inspecting her hand that hand will come in contact with other objects, whereupon the child will grasp these objects, and this experience eventually leads to the child being able to reach for objects when she sees them even though her hand is out of her visual field when she first becomes aware of these objects. When she does this and can reach successfully for the objects that she wants and then inspect what she has in her hand at her leisure, she can then go on to learn about the nature of objects around her. One intriguing possibility that Piaget raises is that this is the way that babies learn about perceptual constancy – the way that they begin to understand that although the size and shape of the visual images of objects which move change all the time, those objects actually retain the same shape and size all the while. Piaget observed that when babies are looking at objects in their hands they often move their hands to and fro at the same time. Thus the visual image changes but the tactual impression that they get at the same time tells the child that the size and shape of the object nevertheless is quite unaltered.

I have dwelt on this particular one of Piaget's observations at some length because it is a telling example of his approach to early development. It illustrates his willingness to ascribe astonishing gaps in the children's understanding of themselves and their environment, and it shows too how, in Piaget's view, children eventually fill such gaps by learning from experiences which they produced for themselves. The baby, Piaget thought, develops by monitoring the results of her own actions.

Let us take up the story again a few weeks later when the baby, now aged 6 months, is adept at reaching for things, at lifting them up and at dropping them, and spends a great deal of time one way or another playing and apparently experimenting with objects. According to Piaget (1954) the baby now understands a great deal about the properties of these objects, but only when she perceives them. She still has no idea of what they are like when they pass out of her perception. Piaget's startling claim was that babies at this age do not realize that objects which have disappeared nevertheless still exist. He based his claim on his observation of what babies did when he showed them an object which they plainly wanted and then, while they were watching, he put it under a cushion or cover which was easily in the baby's reach. Instead of uncovering the object, Piaget observed, babies of 6 months simply turned their attention elsewhere. They are, he argued, in principle quite capable of lifting up the cushion and uncovering the object, but they do not, and that means, in his view, that they simply have not grasped the fact that an object which they can no longer perceive nevertheless continues to exist.

At 9 months or so their behaviour changes. Now they begin quite consistently and successfully to search for the hidden object under the cushion, and you might have thought that that would be the end of the story – that Piaget would have to agree that the infant who searched for the object under a cushion knew that it was there all the time.

Not a bit of it. Piaget found that this age (roughly from 9 to 12 months) babies made a peculiar mistake, which he called the AB error, and he inferred from this error that babies still do not understand the permanence and the independence of objects. The AB error is one of the most surprising patterns of behaviour ever observed in young children, and it is to Piaget's credit that he did not simply dismiss it as a random or trivial bungling of an inexperienced infant. Piaget's observation was that when he hid the object in one place (A) once or twice, the 9-month-old baby retrieved it without hesitation. But when he then put it under another cover in another place (B) the child watched him doing so and then promptly searched at the first location. What can be the reason for this odd reaction?

Piaget's hypothesis is complex and provocative. He argued that at this age the baby misunderstands what is going on when she searches under a cover and retrieves an object which she has seen being hidden there. She still thinks that the object was obliterated when it disappeared, but she also thinks that her action of reaching under the cover had actually recreated or reconstituted the object. In other words she believes in a sort of response-magic. So when she sees the object hidden in another place (B) there is no reason for her to reach to B. To recreate the object, all that she has to do is to repeat the action of reaching to A that has so successfully brought the object back in the past. Thus according to Piaget the AB error demonstrates that even when children search for objects they do not at first understand that the object continues to exist if they can no longer see it.

By the age of 12 months or so the baby no longer makes this mistake, but even then she makes some surprising errors. Piaget now looked for spatial inferences and failed at first to find them. His standard task was to put a toy in a small container and then to move the container underneath a cover and empty it at that point. Then he took the empty container out and allowed the infant to search inside it. The question was 'What would the infant do when she discovered that the object was no longer there?'. The only other possible place where it could be was under the cover, and Piaget wanted to know whether babies could make this simple inference. The answer was that they could not – or at any rate could not until they were 18 months. Then they solved even this task, and this I think is the first logical move that Piaget observed in young children. Only when they make such inferences, he argued, can they really be said to understand the permanence and the independence of the objects around them.

I have chosen two notable examples, but they are only examples, of a vast number of themes which Piaget pursued in his study of the psychological world of the baby – a world which he construed as being almost unimaginably different from ours. But throughout his analysis of the many aspects of behaviour which he studied in children up to 2 years he reiterated one central theme. Babies at this age learn from the results of their own actions, and what they learn is how to act effectively. The intelligence which babies acquire for themselves is, in Piaget's terms, practical intelligence.

This intelligence works well for a 2-year-old but soon it will not be so effective. In Piaget's next major period of development, which he called the period of concrete operations, the child had to acquire the ability not just to act logically but also to make explicit logical judgements.

Before we embark on Piaget's remarkable account of intellectual development from the age of roughly 4 years to roughly 13 years, I should like to make a theoretical point. Piaget looked at children's changing ability to deal with a large number of apparently heterogeneous problems, in all of which he found younger children to be quite at sea and older children to be reasonably competent. But he was saying more than just that the younger children were alogical in their thought processes, though that was certainly his claim. He made as well a deeper theoretical claim, which is that there is an underlying ability of central importance which children have to gain to solve any of the logical problems that he devised for them. This underlying ability he called 'reversibility' (Gold 1987). It means the ability to cancel a change – to retrace one's intellectual footsteps. If I add 4 counters to 5 already there to get 9 I know that at the same time that subtracting 5 will reduce the counters to 4 in number, because I know that if $5 + 4 = 9$ then $9 - 5$ must equal 4. I know this because even though I have mingled the set of 5 with the set of 4 I can simultaneously understand that the total set of 9 consists of two sub-sets, 5 and 4. Simultaneity is extremely important here. It is not a question of dealing with the subsets on one occasion and the total set on the other. Reversibility is the ability to make or to see a change and at exactly the same time to cancel it out in one's head.

We can turn now to some of Piaget's central studies to see how this principle works. By far the most famous and also the most controversial of these is the conservation experiment (Piaget 1952a). The purpose of the conservation task is to test children's understanding of the principle of invariance – which is that a quantity stays the same unless it is added to or subtracted from. Other changes, such as perceptual ones, are irrelevant. So, stretching out a row of counters or bunching them up has no effect whatsoever on its number, but putting a new counter into the row or taking one away does.

The conservation task itself is a two-stage affair. First the child is shown two quantities which are identical in two senses: they are the same in quantity and they look exactly alike. The child is asked to compare them and usually has no difficulty in saying that they are the same in quantity. Then the perceptual appearance of one of the quantities is transformed. Nothing is added to it or taken away, but its perceptual appearance is changed. The child is asked, for a second time, to compare the two quantities. If she understands that nothing has changed because nothing has been added or taken away, then she should say that the two quantities are still the same. But if she does not think that and says that one quantity is greater than the other, she does not understand the invariance principle, according to Piaget.

The results are not in doubt. Indeed they have an extraordinary generality. There cannot be many countries in the world where this oft-repeated experiment has not yet been tried, and it has always produced the same result. Young children do very badly when asked the second question after the perceptual transformation. Older children do much better. To Piaget this means that the understanding of invariance develops during this time. Four-year-old children do not understand it. Ten-year-olds, by and large, do.

The connection that Piaget makes between this task and the notion of reversibility is clear. Piaget's idea was that children eventually understand that nothing apart from the perceptual appearance changes when they see liquid tipped from a fat to a thin container, because they can at the same time make the opposite transformation in their head. By cancelling out the perceptual change they can realize that nothing quantitative actually has changed. The analysis does not seem compelling to me because it could be applied as well to a relevant as to an irrelevant transformation. On the same logic a person who sees an addition to a row of counters and is able to imagine the same number of counters should come to the incorrect conclusion that adding the counters has had no effect on the row's quantity. Simply being able to imagine the opposite transformation does not ensure the understanding of invariance.

Nevertheless, the idea about reversibility proved a powerful one, for it led to a wide variety of other tasks. One of these is the class inclusion task, which is meant to test children's ability to form classes logically. Inhelder and Piaget (1964) wanted to know whether children can divide a major class (flowers) into two or more sub-classes (roses, daffodils) and still realize that, added together, they form the major class. In the task inclusion class he showed children, say, seven roses and three daffodils and asked them whether there were more roses than flowers or more flowers than roses. The younger children answered incorrectly that there are more roses than flowers, from which Piaget deduced that having divided the flowers into roses and daffodils they cannot at the same time (again simultaneity is important) cancel out that division and conceive of the two sub-sets as a major set of flowers.

Reversibility, or rather the lack of it, is also the explanation for children's failure in the transitive inference problem which I have already described and in the seriation problem as well, in which children have to arrange a set of sticks of different size in ascending or descending order. Young children, Piaget claimed, are perfectly able to see that one quantity is smaller or larger than another, but they cannot understand that the same quantity can be at the same time both smaller than one quantity and larger than another. Seeing that the same quantity simultaneously has opposite relations to two different quantities is impossible for the child who cannot manage internal reversals.

It is easy to see why Piaget's concern with reversibility also led him to the study of children's understanding of part–whole relationships and thence of proportions (Piaget and Inhelder 1975). If you have a set of counters some of which have crosses on and others not, and you consider how many have crosses, you cannot work out the proportion of those with crosses to the total number of counters unless you can at the same time consider that total. But an 'irreversible' child, according to Piaget, cannot do that. He cannot divide them into two sections, crosses and no crosses, and at the same time consider the relationship of one section to the whole, because as far as the younger child is concerned the total is quite inaccessible once it has been divided into two or more sub-sections. So Piaget produced a set of tasks which apparently showed that young children are indeed unable to form proportional judgements.

The picture is clear (though incomplete). Piaget has drawn our attention to the sometimes astonishing difficulties that young children have with apparently simple and obvious problems and to the very great changes that take place in children's performance in these tasks as they grow older. At the very least there are appreciable changes in children's intellectual performance in some tasks of central importance.

The significance of these claims hardly needs an explanation. If his idea about the development of the understanding of invariance is right, then there is little that young children can understand about number or about science. A child who thinks that bunching up a row of five counters alters its number plainly does not understand the meaning of number words even if she can count with some proficiency. Similarly a child who does not understand transitivity should not be able to grasp the principles of measurement; and a child who cannot form logical classifications will be at a loss in biology, in history and in geography. But as we shall see, all these claims are disputed.

I have no time, I am afraid, to take Piaget's picture of development further, which is a shame because his third major period of development, which roughly coincides with adolescence, is also one of extraordinary interest. I turn instead to the second major aspect of Piaget's developmental theory – the causal side. I have mentioned already his central idea that children construct their own intellectual development and do so on the basis of their own informal experiences. But the theory is more specific than this.

The idea of equilibration lies at the heart of Piaget's notion of the causes of development (Piaget 1973). For Piaget the main motivation in cognitive behaviour is coherence. Children are happy with their own intellectual strategies so long as these provide consistent and coherent explanations for the events in their lives. But inevitably children are drawn into experiences about which they find they have conflicting views. They are stuck with two mutually conflicting views about the same thing. For example, a child who compares the amount of liquid in a fat and a thin container might think that there is more in the fat container because of its breadth but that there is more in the thin container because the level is higher. It is clear that both judgements cannot be right, and therefore a conflict of this sort is a strong signal that something is wrong with the intellectual system. It leads, according to Piaget, to an unpleasant subjective state which he called disequilibrium. The child is driven to get rid of the state and she does so by altering her intellectual strategies, in such a way that she can now explain such events to herself in a coherent manner. Once this happens equilibrium is restored, at any rate until the child is led into other experiences which produce another conflict, and then the whole process repeats itself. It should be clear why this idea leads to a stage theory. While the child is in equilibrium, she remains at the same stage: when she is thrown into disequilibrium she moves up to the next stage, and so on.

One of the surprising things about this causal theory is how very little evidence there is for it. Piaget himself provided none as far as I can see. His colleagues Inhelder *et al.* (1974) did show that children are helped somewhat in intervention experiments in which there is a conflict between what they expect to happen and what actually does happen, but this is a weak sort of conflict and not on the whole the sort that Piaget was talking about. His interest was in what happens when the child thinks two mutually incompatible things about the same event, and not in the child finding that she had made the wrong prediction.

But this is not the only problem. Another is that it is difficult to see how this causal mechanism could work (Bryant 1990). A conflict is certainly a signal that something is wrong – that the intellectual system is not working properly. So it tells the child that there is a problem, but it does not tell her how to solve it. To find that you think two mutually opposing things about the same event is to know that either one or both of your views are wrong. But that does not tell you what is right and it does not even tell you whether it is one or both views that are wrong. Piaget's conflict is a danger signal, and no more than that.

So far I have described Piaget's work entirely from his own point of view. But a theory that makes such radical and such surprising claims is bound to be controversial, and it is impossible to assess the importance of Piaget's contribution without going into the controversies that surround it.

You will recall that earlier I mentioned three approaches to developmental psychology, one which makes claims for a considerable innate intellectual apparatus, another which stresses the introduction of the child into the culture, and the third – Piaget's – which argues for a radical development of children's underlying intellectual mechanisms. Both of the alternative views have had critical things to say about Piaget's work, but their criticisms differ. The people who argue for the importance of children's innate endowment argue mainly that Piaget's claims are too pessimistic and that many of his most striking results are false negatives: failures on the part of children which are not real failures. On the other hand those who stress the importance of the child's introduction to the culture complain that Piaget simply left out of his scheme a set of cultural experiences of extreme importance.

Let us look now at the first of these two claims about false negatives. First an experimental point: there can be no doubt that despite his experimental ingenuity Piaget was cavalier about the experimental method. I particularly noticed this when I worked in the Genevan department. They had at the time the very good system of discussing in public experiments that they were about to do, and I went to such discussions whenever I could. I noticed that the research workers there would start with a theoretical idea, and a prediction – usually about some task that a child would find difficult. The task that they chose was always ingenious and also to the point, in that if their hypothesis was right then young children should be in difficulties in that task. But that was usually that. They hardly ever went further – by which I mean they never then considered what other possible explanations there might be for the predicted result and what steps they should take to build in controls to ensure that these alternatives were eliminated. In fact the word 'control' did not seem to be part of their vocabulary, and the result was that their experiments were almost always single-condition ones and beset by all the problems that such experiments inevitably pose.

This is a general point. Let us see how it works in practice. What alternative explanations are there for Piaget's striking experimental results? We can start with the baby work and the apparently simple observation that babies seem to lose interest in an attractive object the moment that it is hidden from them. There is an alternative explanation to Piaget's claim that babies think that the object has been obliterated by being put under a cushion. It is that babies understand that the object is still there under the cushion, but do not know what to do about it. They do not realize that the way to get at a covered object is to uncover it.

How does one get round this apparent impasse? One way is to adopt a different – and perhaps more basic – measure of the babies' reactions. It took many years, but first Tom Bower (1971, 1982) and then René Baillargeon (Baillargeon *et al.* 1985; Baillargeon 1986, 1987) came up with the idea of measuring surprise. When babies are surprised they register definite heart-rate changes, and they also look at what is going on appreciably longer than when they are faced with an entirely predictable event. Bower (1971) put a screen in front of an object and then soon after removed the screen. Half the times the object was still there and on the other half it was not. He reported that on the basis of their heart-rate changes the children were more surprised when the object was no longer there than when it was present. He argued, and the argument seems incontrovertible, that the babies had expected the object to be still there and were surprised when it was not.

Baillargeon *et al.* (1985) showed children a block of wood and then raised a drawbridge contraption in front of the object so that it was completely hidden. They then dropped the screen towards the object. Sometimes it stopped at the point where it should have, given that the now invisible block of wood ought to have blocked its path. At other times (by means of a simple conjuring trick) the screen travelled through 180 degrees and ended up flat on the table, which meant that it travelled through space which should have been occupied by the solid block – a surprising event. And it *was* surprising for 4-month-old babies. They looked for a longer time at the impossible event than at the possible one.

It is hard to think of any other explanation for these results than the alternative one that I have offered – the alternative that Piaget did not consider and therefore did not rule out. It seems that very young babies do understand the continued existence of hidden objects. They just do not know what to do about them.

The AB experiment gives us another example of a neglected control. Piaget and many other people assumed that the error must be something to do with object permanence because it occurred in a hiding game. But then George Butterworth (1977) had the very good idea of repeating the experiment with two kinds of task. In one the object was hidden as in Piaget's experiments. The object was hidden first in one opaque box and then in another. But in the other kind of task the object was always visible. It was put in completely transparent boxes (first in A and then in B) and the baby never lost sight of it. Yet Butterworth found, to his surprise and mine, that the error occurred just as much in the transparent condition as in the opaque one. The object need not be hidden for the error to occur. In many ways this last result makes the error even more interesting, because it seems even more bizarre. Why does the baby search in one place when the object is plainly in view in another?

These results certainly throw a great deal of doubt on Piaget's ideas about object permanence. Notice, however, that the dispute is a productive one. Even if Piaget's claims were wrong, his ideas have led to research which has thrown up some interesting and even now quite surprising results. That on its own is a notable contribution.

The controversies about Piaget's work on older children are more acrimonious, and yet it is my impression that many of his ideas about these children have survived rather better than his ideas about infants. But we need to take the various techniques separately, because there is a different story to be told about each of them. I will concentrate on conservation and on transitivity.

The main objection to the conservation experiment is an alternative suggested by Donaldson (1978, 1982), by Rose and Blank (1974) and by Light *et al.* (1979). It takes the form of a suggestion that the whole experiment in its traditional form is in fact a gigantic misunderstanding between the experimenter and the child. These people argue that the child is puzzled about the purpose of the adult experimenter and anxious to give the right answer to his or her questions. The experimenter asks an easy question in the first part of the experiment, then makes the perceptual change, and then asks the same question for the second time. The child reasons that because the experimenter has made a change and then immediately asks the same question as before this change, she now needs a new answer. 'If he has made a change then I too must change my answer' is the reasoning that Donaldson attributes to the young child.

How does one test this alternative? The experiment by McGarrigle and Donaldson (1974) is certainly the best-known attempt to do so. They compared two conditions. One was the standard conservation procedure. The experimenter himself conducted the experiment throughout, asked both questions, and carried out the transformation in all seriousness. In the other condition – which was called the accidental condition – the procedure was different, in that the transformation was made by a marauding teddy bear. What happened was that the experimenter asked the first question, and then introduced the child to an extremely active teddy bear which moved around and as though by accident changed the appearance of one of the rows. Then the teddy bear was put away, and the adult asked the child to compare the rows once again.

The results were startling. The children produced many more correct answers in the accidental condition than in the standard task. The experimenters argued that this meant that the children understood the invariance principle and used it in the accidental condition when they thought that the perceptual change was nothing to do with the experimenter. Their performance in the standard condition was, according to this argument, a definite underestimate of their understanding of invariance.

This result and others like it have had a very great effect. They have been at the heart of a growing belief that Piaget's ideas are passé. But there are reasons now for believing that the McGarrigle and Donaldson experiment might itself have been misleading. One possible criticism of it is that in the accidental condition the children might not have even noticed the perceptual change so casually made by the teddy bear, because they were so taken with its other antics. There is now some evidence to support this idea. Moore and Frye (1986) repeated the McGarrigle and Donaldson task, but they also introduced other tasks in which either the adult or the teddy bear actually added a counter to one of the rows. The children were much more likely to say (incorrectly) that there was no change in the number of counters when the teddy bear did the addition than when the adult did it. In other words it seems that the main effect of the teddy bear was to distract the child from paying attention to the transformations, whether these were merely perceptual or really changed the number.

The view that Piaget might after all be right about conservation is bolstered by another experiment by Miller (1982), who eliminated the experimenter completely when it came to the transformation. He introduced into a conservation test naturally occurring transformations which were apparently not engineered by the experimenter at all. Insects spread out in one condition, boats in another. No one pushed them, they just scurried or floated apart. Yet the children had just as much difficulty in these tasks as in the traditional versions of the conservation task where the experimenter did all the moving. There was no difference at all between the two conditions. Here, at any rate, the children's speculations about the experimenters' purposes seemed to play no part.

The complaints about the transitive inference experiment have had as chequered a fate. The strongest objection was raised by Tom Trabasso and myself (Bryant and Trabasso 1971; Bryant 1974). We argued that children may fail this task not for logical reasons but simply because they cannot remember the premises, and we introduced a task in which we ensured that children did remember these premises reasonably well. We found that under these conditions even 4-year-old children made the transitive inference correctly, and that the few failures that they made could be readily attributed to these few memory failures.

But this conclusion, I readily admit, is quite controversial, and there are many people who argue that the precautions that we took to make sure that the children remembered the premises might have had the quite unintended effect of training them how to make inferences (Perner and Mansbridge 1983). The question is still unresolved, and I certainly cannot claim now as I claimed once that we had proved Piaget wrong on one of his central claims about school-age children, although some recent work of ours (Pears and Bryant 1990) appears to show that 4-year-old children can make transitive inferences about spatial position even when no great memory load and therefore no memory training is involved.

The criticisms levelled at Piaget's theory from the other alternative viewpoint – that intellectual development consists of a gradual introduction to the culture – are less detailed. Mostly the complaints are about his omissions. Piaget stuck as closely as he could to logic: when he wrote about cultural inventions it was mainly to show that children's logical failings often prevented them from understanding how these worked. One good example, I think, is of Piaget's approach to measurement. He simply had no truck with standard units – such as centimetres or kilograms – and announced very firmly that to study children's understanding of these would be a trivial waste of time. One had to stick to logic, and in this case to transitive inference. That, he thought, was where the crucial development lay. With number too he simply ignored the counting system. Yet numbers are organized into decades, decades into hundreds, and so on, and surely we ought to find out how children come across with this structural system.

Still, it is probably very tough and utterly churlish to complain that Piaget left something out of his research when he managed to do much more research than anyone else has. And in a way the most serious disagreement that this school of thought has with Piaget's ideas is over an issue for which neither group has any decent evidence at all. I refer once again to the question of the causes of development. Vygotsky (Vygotsky 1986; Vygotsky and Luria 1993) argued strongly for the influence of language on development. Others from a similar point of view have claimed that literacy (Olson *et al.* 1985), or numeracy (Fuson 1988; Saxe 1991; Nunes *et al.* 1993), or experience with computers (Papert 1980) transform people's intellectual processes; and maybe they do. But we simply cannot be sure, because we have not got enough evidence yet. Piaget firmly rejected the possibility that these were powerful influences in behaviour, because they are external and Piaget thought that the main causes of intellectual change were internal – the child working things out for herself. But Piaget too had too little evidence for this radical view, and we still do not know one way or the other what to say about this, the most important of developmental disputes.

To summarize: Piaget was a very great developmental psychologist whose influence on the subject surpasses anyone else's. One of his main contributions was to demonstrate how easy and rewarding it is to do simple experiments on young children's understanding of quite subtle complex topics. His theory – that logic develops, that it is the product not the engine of development – is controversial; but he was right to raise these claims, and developmental psychology is a better subject for his having done so. The greatest problem about his theory is his idea of the causes of intellectual development. We are very far from knowing how justified is his idea about internal conflict as the main engine of development. We do not even know yet how to test the idea properly – and to compare it with its competitors. And while we wonder what to do about Piaget's internal conflict perhaps we should remember the great poet Yeats' remark, 'We make out of arguments with others, politics, and out of arguments with ourselves, poetry.' Perhaps the conflicts that Piaget talked so much about had more to do with artistic than with logical mathematical skills. We shall see, or at any rate I hope that we shall see.

REFERENCES

Baillargeon, R. (1986) 'Representing the existence and the location of hidden objects in 6- and 8-month-old infants', *Cognition* 23: 21–52.
—— (1987) 'Young infants' reasoning about the physical and spatial characteristics of a hidden object', *Cognitive Development* 2: 179–200.
Baillargeon, R., Spelke, S. and Wasserman, S. (1985) 'Object permanence in five-month-old infants', *Cognition* 20: 191–208.
Bower, T.G.R. (1971) 'Objects in the world of the infant', *Scientific American* 225: 30–8.
—— (1982) *Development in Infancy*, 2nd edn, New York: W.H. Freeman.
Bryant, P.E. (1974) *Perception and Understanding in Young Children*, London: Methuen.
—— (1990) 'Empirical evidence for causes in development', in G. Butterworth and P. Bryant, *Causes of Development: Interdisciplinary Perspectives*, Hemel Hempstead: Harvester Wheatsheaf.
Bryant, P.E. and Trabasso, T. (1971) 'Transitive inferences and memory in young children', *Nature* 232: 456–8.
Butterworth, G. (1977) 'Object disappearance and error in Piaget's stage IV task', *Journal of Experimental Child Psychology* 23: 391–501.
Donaldson, M. (1978) *Children's Minds*, London: Fontana.
—— (1982) 'Conservation: what is the question?', *British Journal of Psychology* 73: 199–207.
Fuson, K.C. (1988) *Children's Counting and Concepts of Number*, New York: Springer-Verlag.
Gelman, R. and Gallistel, C.R. (1978) *The Child's Understanding of Number*, Cambridge, Mass.: Harvard University Press.
Gold, R. (1987) *The Description of Cognitive Development: Three Piagetian Themes*, Oxford: Clarendon Press.
Inhelder, B. and Piaget, J. (1964) *The Early Growth of Logic in the Child*, London: Routledge and Kegan Paul.
Inhelder, B., Sinclair, H. and Bovet, M. (1974) *Learning and the Development of Cognition*, London: Routledge and Kegan Paul.
Johnson, M.H. and Morton, J. (1991) *Biology and Cognitive Development*, Oxford: Blackwell.

Light, P.H., Buckingham, N. and Robbins, A.H. (1979) 'The conservation task as an interactional setting', British Journal of Educational Psychology 49: 304–10.

McGarrigle, J. and Donaldson, M. (1974) 'Conservation accidents', Cognition 3: 341–50.

Miller, S. (1982) 'On the generalisability of conservation: a comparison of different types of transformation', British Journal of Psychology 73: 221–30.

Moore, C. and Frye, D. (1986) 'The effect of the experimenter's intention on the child's understanding of conservation', Cognition 22: 283–98.

Nunes, T., Schliemann, A.-L.and Carraher, D. (1993) Street Mathematics and School Mathematics, New York: Cambridge University Press.

Olson, D.R., Torrance, N. and Hildyard, A. (1985) Literacy, Language and Learning, Cambridge: Cambridge University Press.

Papert, S. (1980) Mindstorms: Children, Computers and Powerful Ideas, Brighton: Harvester Press.

Pears, R. and Bryant, P. (1990) 'Transitive inferences by young children about spatial position', British Journal of Psychology 81: 497–510.

Perner, J. and Mansbridge, D.G. (1983) 'Developmental differences in encoding length series', Child Development 54: 710–19.

Piaget, J. (1921) 'Une forme verbale de la comparaison chez l'enfant', Archives de Psychologie 18: 141–72.

—— (1952a) The Child's Conception of Number, London: Routledge and Kegan Paul.

—— (1952b) The Origins of Intelligence, London: Routledge and Kegan Paul.

—— (1954) The Construction of Reality in the Child, London: Routledge and Kegan Paul.

—— (1973) The Child's Conception of the World, London: Paladin.

Piaget, J. and Inhelder, B. (1963) The Child's Conception of Space, London: Routledge and Kegan Paul.

—— (1975) The Origin of the Idea of Chance in Children, London: Routledge and Kegan Paul.

Piaget, J., Inhelder, B. and Szeminska, A. (1960) The Child's Conception of Geometry, London: Routledge and Kegan Paul.

Rose, S. and Blank, M. (1974) 'The potency of context in children's cognition: an illustration through conservation', Child Development 45: 499–502.

Saxe, G.B. (1991) Culture and Cognitive Development: Studies in Mathematical Understanding, Hillsdale, NJ: Erlbaum.

Spelke, E.S., Breinlinger, K., Macomber, J. and Jacobson, K. (1992) 'Origins of knowledge', Psychological Review 99: 605–32.

Starkey, P., Spelke, E.S. and Gelman, R. (1990) 'Numerical abstraction by human infants', Cognition 36: 97–128.

van der Veer, R. and Valsiner, J. (1991) Understanding Vygotsky, Oxford: Blackwell.

Vygotsky, L.S. (1986) Thought and Language, Cambridge, Mass.: MIT Press.

Vygotsky, L.S. and Luria, A.R. (1993) *Studies on the History of Behavior: Ape, Primitive and Child*, Hillsdale, NJ: Erlbaum.

Index

Darwin, Charles 1, 2, 51, 60, 68,
71, 113–14; *The Origin of Species*
6
Darwin, Violetta 2
daydreaming 30–6, 63, 64, 65
death instinct 51, 55, 56
depression (melancholia) 41, 57,
70
determinism 48, 112
developmental psychology 133–52;
varying approaches to 132–3,
145; *see also* children,
development of
disequilibrium 144
displacement activity 88
display movements 87–8
dominant psychological motives
27
Donahoe, J.W. 114
Donaldson, M. 148–9
'Dora' 67
dreams 31, 63, 65–7; night 36; *see
also* daydreaming
drugs and alcohol 31, 39–40
dualism 55
Dublin 24, 44
ducks, 87, 90

education 100, 120
efference copy 85
ego 61, 62
Einstein, Albert 63
electroencephalograph 65
emotion 22, 23, 26, 36, 41–2; and
reason 61–2
energy models of motivation 93,
95; *see also* hydraulic model
enthusiasm 97
environment: and behaviour 112,
113; and heredity 8–9, 94
environmental concerns 101
epistemology, evolutionary 99
equilibration 143–4
Eros instinct 55, 56
ethology 76, 77–105;
rapprochement with comparative
psychology 93–4, 95
Eton College 13
eugenics 2, 10–11, 81, 97
evolution 95, 114

exploration 100, 101
exploratory drive 60–1
eye-shift patterns 31

factor-analytic studies 30–1
fantasies 31, 35–6
father, slaughter of 68
Field, Nigel 41
fingerprints 1, 12–13
First World War 59
fish 83, 84, 89, 101; cichlid 86–7
fixed action pattern (FAP) 82–3,
84, 87, 89–90, 96
flashbacks 31
Fliess, W. 53
Folia Biotheoretica 75
folk psychology 99
Forster, E.M. 62
Frankfurt, Goethe prize 50, 52
Frazer, Sir James, *The Golden
Bough* 68
free association 15, 70–1
freedom 122–3
Freiberg 48
Freud, Anna 50
Freud, Jacob and Amalie 48
Freud, Martha (Bernays) 48, 50,
51
Freud, Sigmund 15, 22, 27, **49–73**,
83, *Plate 3*; and anthropology 51,
68; appearance 53; and art and
literature 50, 53, 63, 72; clinical
descriptions 69–70; as collector
of antiquities 54; dream theory
65–7; illness 48, 52, 54; influence
of 51–2, 69–71; intolerance 54–5;
and medicine 48, 50;
obsessionality 50, 53–7;
overgeneralization 64;
personality 50, 53–5;
productivity 52, 53; prose style
52; revision of theories 54, 55;
and smoking 54;
superstitiousness 54; technique
of treatment 69, 70; and women
51; autobiography 50–1;
Civilization and Its Discontents 56;
'The disposition to obsessional
neurosis' 53; *The Future of an
Illusion* 56–7; *The Interpretation of*

162   *Index*